The Passionate Preaching *of*

Martyn Lloyd-Jones

The Long Line of Godly Men Profiles
Series editor, Steven J. Lawson

A Long Line of Godly Men Profile

The Passionate Preaching *of*

Martyn Lloyd-Jones

STEVEN J. LAWSON

R *Reformation Trust* A DIVISION OF LIGONIER MINISTRIES, ORLANDO, FL

The Passionate Preaching of Martyn Lloyd-Jones

© 2016 by Steven J. Lawson

Published by Reformation Trust Publishing
a division of Ligonier Ministries
421 Ligonier Court, Sanford, FL 32771
Ligonier.org   ReformationTrust.com

Printed in Crawfordsville, Indiana
RR Donnelley and Sons
February 2016
First edition

Cover illustration: Steven Noble
Interior design and typeset: Katherine Lloyd, The DESK

Library of Congress Cataloging-in-Publication Data

Names: Lawson, Steven J., author.
Title: The passionate preaching of Martyn Lloyd-Jones / Steven J. Lawson.
Description: First edition. | Orlando, FL : Reformation Trust Publishing, 2015. | Series: A long line of Godly men profile
Identifiers: LCCN 2015042345 | ISBN 9781567696387
Subjects: LCSH: Lloyd-Jones, David Martyn. | Clergy--Great Britain--Biography. | Preaching--Great Britain--History--20th century.
Classification: LCC BX4827.L68 L39 2015 | DDC 251.0092--dc23
LC record available at http://lccn.loc.gov/2015042345

This book is fondly dedicated to my brother
Dr. Mark A. Lawson
a devoted Christian, gifted physician,
and lover of British history,
who first encouraged me
to put these church history
and theological studies
into print in this
Long Line of Godly Men Profiles series

TABLE OF CONTENTS

Followers Worthy to Be Followed

Down through the centuries, God has raised up a long line of godly men whom He has mightily used at strategic moments in church history. These valiant individuals have come from all walks of life, from the ivy-covered halls of elite schools to the dusty back rooms of tradesmen's shops. They have arisen from all points of this world, from highly visible venues in densely populated cities to obscure hamlets in remote locations. Yet despite these differences, these pivotal figures have had much in common.

Each man possessed an unwavering faith in the Lord Jesus Christ, but more than that, each of these stalwarts of the faith believed deeply in the God-exalting truths known as the doctrines of grace. Though they differed in secondary matters of theology, they stood shoulder to shoulder in embracing these biblical teachings that magnify the sovereign grace of God in salvation. These spiritual leaders upheld the foundational truth that "salvation is of the Lord."[1]

Any survey of church history reveals that those who have embraced these Reformed truths have been granted extraordinary confidence in their God. Far from paralyzing these spiritual giants, the doctrines of grace kindled within their hearts a reverential awe for God that humbled their souls before His throne. The truths of divine sovereignty emboldened these men to rise up and advance the cause of Christ on the earth. With an enlarged vision for the expansion of His kingdom upon the earth, they stepped forward boldly to accomplish the work of ten, even twenty men. They arose with wings like eagles and soared over their times. The doctrines of grace empowered them to serve God in their divinely appointed hour of history, leaving a godly inheritance for future generations.

This Long Line of Godly Men Profiles series highlights key figures in the agelong procession of these sovereign-grace men. The purpose of this series is to explore how these significant figures used their God-given gifts and abilities to impact their times and further the work of Christ. Because they were courageous followers of the Lord, their examples are worthy of emulation today.

This volume focuses on the man who is regarded as most responsible for reestablishing expository preaching in

---

1. Ps. 3:8; Jonah 2:9.

major parts of the church in the twenty-first century, Martyn Lloyd-Jones. This soul-arresting expositor, who ministered in Westminster Chapel, London, reintroduced a new generation to the Puritans, the Great Awakening, and Reformed theology. It was Lloyd-Jones who revitalized biblical preaching in a day when the spiritual impetus of many pulpits in England was far too commonly absent. The Doctor stood in his strategic pulpit and preached with a spiritual force that had been long absent in the church. Lloyd-Jones stands as an example of what God can do through a man who honors and heralds His Word. He is worthy of our consideration in the pages that follow.

Before we proceed, I want to thank the publishing team at Reformation Trust for their commitment to this Long Line of Godly Men Profiles series. I remain thankful for the ongoing influence of my former professor and current friend, Dr. R.C. Sproul. I must also express my gratitude to Chris Larson, who is so instrumental in overseeing this series. I want to thank Kevin Gardner for his editing of this work.

Moreover, I am indebted to the staff of OnePassion Ministries, who have undergirded my efforts to produce this book. I want to express my gratitude for my executive ministry assistant, Kay Allen, who typed this document, and Dustin Benge, director of operations at OnePassion Ministries, who helped prepare this manuscript. Without their skillful help, this book would not be in your hands.

I thank God for my family, who support me in my preaching and writing ministry. My wife, Anne, has made enormous sacrifices and given much support to allow me to do what God has called me to do. Heaven will reveal this. Our four adult children, Andrew, James, Grace Anne, and John, remain pillars of strength for me in this work.

May the Lord use this book to embolden a new generation of believers to bring its witness for Jesus Christ upon this world for God. Through this profile of Martyn Lloyd-Jones, may you be strengthened to walk in a manner worthy of your calling. May you be zealous in your study of the written Word of God for the exaltation of Christ and the advance of His kingdom. And for those of you who preach, may you do so with "logic on fire."

Soli Deo gloria!
—Steven J. Lawson
Series editor

The Doctor's Mantle

The thriving metropolis of London is a city that holds much allure for anyone who loves church history. Within this vast urban center are many remembrances of a glorious past for Christianity. Every time I travel to London, I am energized by the many places where spiritual heroes of the faith once lived and died. Many even gave their lives in martyrdom on this English soil for the advance of the gospel around the world.

Particularly, I am drawn to Bunhill Fields, where many notable Puritans were buried, including John Bunyan (d. 1688), John Owen (1616–83), and Isaac Watts (1674–1748). Nearby is Smithfield, where the first martyr burned by Bloody Mary, John Rogers (c. 1500–1555), was executed. Whitehall Gardens contains the imposing statue of the Father of the English Bible, William Tyndale (1494–1536).

The British Library houses only a fragment, known as the Cologne fragment, of the 1525 Tyndale New Testament and a rare 1526 edition. Northwood Cemetery is where the body of the prince of preachers, Charles Spurgeon (1834–92), was laid to rest.

On a recent preaching trip to London, there was one site that I had not yet visited that remained a must. I had to go to Westminster Chapel, where David Martyn Lloyd-Jones once preached and influenced the evangelical world. Taking the subway, I made my way on foot to this historic building, only a short walk from Buckingham Palace. Upon approaching the chapel on street level, I felt as though I was stepping back in time. The facade of the chapel remains exactly as it was during the days of the Doctor, complete with its landmark tower.

Several knocks on the door yielded no response. But persistence paid off when a maintenance man answered and allowed me entrance. He led me into the sanctuary, where for thirty years Lloyd-Jones had expounded the Word of God. I stepped onto the platform and turned around to look at the pews to see what it was like to stand where the Doctor had once stood as he preached so faithfully. I gazed up into a two-tiered balcony that wraps around the entire sanctuary, as though a cloud of witnesses encircles the pulpit on every side. The sight was awe-inspiring, and since I am a preacher, the sheer sight made me want to preach.

At the rear of the platform was the pulpit from which

Lloyd-Jones once preached. No longer in use, the sacred desk is relegated to a back place, out of view. I approached the pulpit and laid my hands upon it. The janitor could tell that I was enraptured by this discovery, so he asked if I would like to see the vestry where the Doctor received inquirers after he preached. I immediately said yes.

He led me behind the pulpit area, and we walked through a door into a plain, unadorned room with only a small desk and chair for furniture. Hanging above the desk on the wall was a picture of the great English preacher Charles Haddon Spurgeon. I could imagine the Doctor in a room very similar to this as he graciously received visitors who wanted to speak with him.

My guide asked if I would like to see the preaching Bible that Lloyd-Jones used. I, of course, answered in the affirmative. He brought out what was to me one of the crown jewels of England, the very pulpit Bible from which the Doctor had expounded the truth. I sat at his desk and opened its pages to Romans 1. My mind raced back to the distinguished sermon series he delivered through Romans, a fourteen-year series that reshaped the landscape of evangelical preaching—a series that he had delivered from this very Bible.

The janitor then asked if I would like to see the black Genevan gown that Lloyd-Jones wore in the pulpit. This was more that my soul could take. In the closet, there was draped on a hanger the actual gown worn by this small Welshman. The janitor pulled it out and before I could think to exercise self-restraint, I asked if I could put it on. Caught off guard, he agreed to allow me to wear it.

In that moment, my thoughts flew back to the time when Spurgeon was traveling through Europe and came to Geneva, Switzerland, where the great magisterial Reformer John Calvin had preached. Spurgeon's hosts asked him if he would like to wear Calvin's black preaching gown. He was hesitant to decline since he did not want to quench their enthusiasm. The Reformer's gown was brought out and placed upon Spurgeon's broad shoulders. The great London preacher remarked it was one of the great moments of his life. I felt much the same, wearing the Doctor's robe.

Here I was in Westminster Chapel, sitting at Lloyd-Jones' desk, wearing his robe, opening his pulpit Bible, staring at the first chapter of Romans, where his finger once pointed as he preached the Word. In this grand moment, I was hoping that something of this great Welshman would rub off on me. Then my thoughts went to this book I was scheduled to write on Lloyd-Jones. I longed that through these pages on the Doctor, then yet to be written, God would be pleased to place the mantle of Lloyd-Jones upon a new generation of preachers.

This book on Lloyd-Jones focuses upon the life and preaching of this incredible man. I pray that God will use it to light a fire in your soul to fulfill His call upon your life.

The hour is upon us for faithful men of God to step into pulpits around the world and preach the Word. The need has never been greater. In a day that clamors for churches to capitulate to the spirit of the age and use entertainment in order to draw crowds, the primacy of biblical preaching must be restored wherever the people of God gather to worship. As it was the need in the time of Lloyd-Jones, so it remains the need today for preachers to herald the Word in the power of the Holy Spirit in order to feed the flock and evangelize the lost.

May the life and ministry of David Martyn Lloyd-Jones serve as an inspiration to your soul that you would give yourself to whatever God has called you to do. No sacrifice will be too great in order to fulfill the good works He has given you to accomplish.

Soli Deo gloria!
Steven J. Lawson
Dallas
August 2015

CHAPTER ONE

A Life
on Fire

Martyn Lloyd-Jones was without question the finest biblical expositor of the twentieth century. In fact, when the final chapter of church history is written, I believe the Doctor will stand as one of the greatest preachers of all time.[1]

—JOHN MACARTHUR

A diminutive figure, short and compact, entered the pulpit at Westminster Chapel in London, wearing a common black Genevan gown. More than two thousand people made their way to the chapel each Lord's Day to listen to a lengthy exposition of Scripture by this renowned preacher from Wales. There were no gimmicks, no theatrics, no entertainment to attract the crowds. There were no testimonies from famous

---

1. Quoted on the back cover of *The Christ-Centered Preaching of Martyn Lloyd-Jones: Classic Sermons for the Church Today*, edited by Elizabeth Catherwood and Christopher Catherwood (Wheaton, Ill.: Crossway, 2014).

personalities to hold the people. There were no dramatic performances. There was a worshiping and praying congregation eager to hear God's man preach the unsearchable riches of God's Word.

At this time, biblical preaching was regarded as irrelevant. Yet, this fiery Welshman addressed this large congregation three times per week with a commanding authority not his own. He expounded the Bible twice on Sunday and once on Friday evening, each time bringing men face-to-face with the glory of God. Through his preaching, souls were brought low and then lifted up. Sins were exposed and grace was extended. People were converted and lives transformed. Because of his penetrating exposition, this formidable figure came to be widely regarded in his time as "the greatest preacher in Christendom."[2] The preacher was David Martyn Lloyd-Jones.

Affectionately known as "the Doctor," this physician-turned-preacher became arguably the foremost expositor of the twentieth century. "There is little doubt," Scottish preacher Eric J. Alexander writes, "that Dr. Martyn Lloyd-Jones was the greatest preacher the English-speaking world has seen in the twentieth century."[3] His pulpit's strategic location in London and the global distribution of his

---

2. Wilbur M. Smith, *Moody Monthly* (October 1955): 32; as quoted by Iain H. Murray, *D. Martyn Lloyd-Jones: The Fight of Faith, 1939–1981* (Edinburgh, Scotland: Banner of Truth, 1990), 329.

3. Eric J. Alexander, foreword to *The Cross: God's Way of Salvation*, by Martyn Lloyd-Jones (Wheaton, Ill.: Crossway, 1986), vii.

printed sermons meant that the influence of the message preached by Lloyd-Jones extended far beyond his city, to the evangelical church in Britain and eventually around the world. Many trace the modern-day resurgence in Reformed theology to the direct influence of Lloyd-Jones' preaching at Westminster.

Affirming this dynamic impact, Peter Lewis writes: "In the history of the pulpit in Britain, the preaching of Martyn Lloyd-Jones is outstanding. He takes his place in a long line of great preachers since the Protestant Reformation, who have stood for the reformation and renewal of the church, the evangelization and awakening of the world."[4] Amidst the spiritual decline in post-World War II England, this gifted expositor stood in the minority in his commitment to biblical preaching. More than any other individual, Lloyd-Jones is most directly responsible for the recovery of true biblical preaching during the latter half of the twentieth century, and the effects of his ministry continue to this day.

Given such a luminous legacy, certain questions must be asked: Who was this twentieth-century British preacher? What characterized his prolific life and ministry? What were the forces that shaped his preaching? What distinguished his expository preaching? What can we learn from his pulpit ministry? In order to answer these questions, we begin in this chapter with an overview of the life of Lloyd-Jones.

---

4. Peter Lewis, "The Doctor as a Preacher," in *Martyn Lloyd-Jones: Chosen by God*, ed. Christopher Catherwood (Westchester, Ill.: Crossway, 1986), 92–93.

Welsh Born and Raised

David Martyn Lloyd-Jones was born December 20, 1899, in Cardiff, Wales. He was the second of three sons to Welsh-speaking parents. His parents, Henry and Magdalen, lived a simple, hardworking life. In 1906, the family moved to Llangeitho, a small village in Cardiganshire (now Ceredigion), in South Wales, where his father ran the local general store. There, his family joined the Calvinistic Methodist church that had been established by Daniel Rowland, one of the fiery preachers of the Welsh revival during the eighteenth century. In this distinctly Reformed denomination, Lloyd-Jones was introduced to the transcendent truths of the sovereignty of God over all of life. Though he was not yet converted, this initial exposure began laying the foundation for a God-centered worldview. The Calvinistic Methodists had a history of great preachers and revivals, which sparked a lifelong interest in church history and spiritual awakenings.

Intellectually brilliant, the young Lloyd-Jones proved to be an exceptional child. Possessing a contemplative side, his boyhood studies produced in him an early love of reading. At age eleven, he won a scholarship to Tregaron County Intermediate School in a nearby town. Young David, later known as Martyn, left home each Monday morning in order to attend school, returning home each Friday evening. He grew in his love of history, a passion that would later develop into a study of the Puritans and the subsequent eras of revival.

4

THE MOVE TO LONDON

In 1914, financial hardship hit the Lloyd-Jones family as bankruptcy forced them to relocate to London. There, his father borrowed money and bought a dairy business, and the family maintained their residence on Regency Street. As providence would have it, the business was in Westminster in central London, the very place where Martyn would later pastor.

Young Martyn rose each morning at 5:30 and delivered milk to local homes. Each day, he walked past Westminster Chapel. The family was invited by some of their customers to attend the chapel, but instead they chose to attend the local Welsh Calvinistic Methodist church, Charing Cross Road Chapel.

On the first Sunday, they sat in front of the family of a successful eye surgeon, Dr. Thomas Phillips, whose daughter, Bethan, Martyn would later marry. Bethan was a medical student at University College Hospital. She was well educated at London University and had distinguished herself by being one of the first women to study medicine at University College Hospital. Her strong character would prove to be an enormous asset to Lloyd-Jones in his future work. With Bethan at his side, it appeared that Lloyd-Jones was poised for a successful career in the field of medicine.

For the next several years, Martyn attended the well-known boys' school St. Marylebone Grammar School, where he completed his preparatory studies. Through all this early education, God was giving him the tools for a lifetime of inquisitive study of the Bible and church history. Upon completing his prescribed course of study, Lloyd-Jones pursued his passion to study medicine in order to prepare to be a physician. At age sixteen, he was accepted into the highly acclaimed training program at St. Bartholomew's Hospital, one of the leading teaching hospitals in England. At age twenty-one, Martyn earned the bachelor of medicine and of surgery, with distinction. He then became a member of the Royal College of Surgeons (1921) and a licentiate of the Royal College of Physicians (1921). At every step, Lloyd-Jones distinguished himself as an outstanding intellect with a bright future as a gifted physician. By his early twenties, Lloyd-Jones stood on the threshold of an extraordinary career in the medical profession.

A DISTINGUISHED YOUNG PHYSICIAN

Lloyd-Jones' abilities in diagnosing illnesses came to the attention of one of the most renowned teachers at St. Bart's Hospital, the eminent Sir Thomas Horder. Horder practiced on London's famous Harley Street, the most distinguished address in British medicine. Further, he was the personal physician to King George V and the royal family. It was no small honor that Horder chose Martyn to become his junior house physician. Eventually, Horder would give Lloyd-Jones the position of chief clinical assistant at the hospital in 1923.

That same year, Martyn earned the highly respected doctorate of medicine from London University at the unusually young age of twenty-three. Next, Lloyd-Jones was awarded the Baillie Research Scholarship (1924) for eighteen months in order to investigate the Pell-Epstein type of Hodgkin's disease (Lymphadenoma).[5] This recognition gained him yet further distinction.

At age twenty-four, Martyn became the first individual to receive research aid from the St. John Harmsworth Memorial Research Fund, to study a heart condition known as infective endocarditis. The results of his study were published in a highly respected medical journal and are now held in the National Library of Wales. At age twenty-five, Martyn became a member of the Royal College of Physicians (1925). Sir James Patterson Ross, president of the Royal College of Surgeons, referred to Lloyd-Jones as "one of the finest clinicians I have ever encountered." By all accounts, the medical career of Lloyd-Jones was soaring to meteoric heights.

5. Philip H. Eveson, personal correspondence with the author, August 10, 2015. "This may have been the subject of his research that led to his MD (Doctor of Medicine) degree but that cannot be proven, as there is no record of his research either in the library of St. Bart's or the University of London. This was before he received research aid from the St John Harmsworth Memorial Research Fund to study a heart condition known as infective endocarditis, study that he completed just prior to his entering the ministry. His research results were not, to my knowledge, published in a medical journal, but as an appendix to a book by C.B. Perry entitled *Bacterial Endocarditis* (Bristol, England: Wright & Sons, 1936). It records his initial experiments, which are to be found in notebooks held at the National Library of Wales in Aberystwyth, not a medical journal."

CONVERTED AND CALLED

Despite these significant achievements, Lloyd-Jones was unhappy. Life seemed fleeting and empty to him. Earlier, at age eighteen, Martyn had been sobered by the death of his brother Harold. His father died when Martyn was twenty-two. Amid these losses, God began to convict him of personal sin and his guilt before God. Though a very religious person, Martyn realized he was spiritually dead. Though outwardly he lived a moral life, he realized this was simply a facade, a mere attempt to put on a respectable front. He saw his desperate need for a true relationship with Jesus Christ. No exact date can be assigned to his conversion, but Lloyd-Jones, age twenty-five, was born again. He later described this turning point in his life:

> For many years I thought I was a Christian when in fact I was not. It was only later that I came to see that I had never been a Christian and became one. . . . What I needed was preaching that would convict me of sin. . . . But I never heard this. The preaching we had was always based on the assumption that we were all Christians.[6]

---

6. Iain H. Murray, *D. Martyn Lloyd-Jones: The First Forty Years, 1899–1939* (Edinburgh, Scotland: Banner of Truth, 1982), 58.

This conversion experience would have a profound effect upon his preaching in the years to come. In the pulpit, Lloyd-Jones would always be doing the work of an evangelist. He knew what it was to be in church but not be in Christ.

CALLED TO PREACH

Newly converted, Lloyd-Jones became convinced that the greatest need of his patients lay far deeper than their physical ailments. He now understood that anyone apart from God is spiritually dead. He realized that he was healing his patients so that they could return to a life of sin. For the next two years, Martyn was embroiled in a deep struggle over how he should invest his life. He lost twenty pounds as he wrestled with whether God was calling him into the ministry.

In June 1926, he made the life-altering decision to leave his medical career in order to pursue what he believed to be the highest calling: the call to preach. He wrote in a letter: "I want to preach . . . and am determined to preach. The precise nature of my future activities remains to be settled, but nothing can or will prevent my going about to tell people of the good news."[7] Once this decision was made, Martyn never looked back.

This change of profession by Lloyd-Jones caused no small sensation in the medical field. That this young, brilliant

---

7. Ibid., 104.

physician would leave a successful and advancing medical career in order to enter the ministry was shocking to most. This new pursuit was made in a day when the advances of modern-day science seemed to be contradicting the claims of the ancient Bible. No intelligent, well-educated person would leave medicine for mere myths, they reasoned. However, Lloyd-Jones was gripped with an unwavering confidence in the Scripture and a need to proclaim its gospel truth regardless of what people thought.

Martyn chose not to pursue a formal seminary education due to the theological liberalism that had infected the British universities. He believed he was divinely gifted by God to fulfill the task to which he had been called and had no need of formal education that compromised Scripture.

In June 1926, Martyn proposed to Bethan Phillips. Though she had many suitors, he won the hand of this beautiful woman. The two were married on January 8, 1927, at Charing Cross Chapel, London. Martyn then faced yet another major decision: Where would he serve the Lord? Though he had cared for many of the London elite, he desired to minister among the poor in his homeland of Wales. Lloyd-Jones traveled there to pursue ministry opportunities but was rebuffed. To the Welsh church officials, a Harley Street doctor serving the working class hardly seemed like a good fit. However, Martyn persevered in what he believed to be the call of God upon his life. On Christmas 1926, he accepted the call to be a pastor in a financially deprived area of South Wales.

Ministering in Wales

Leaving the bright lights of London, Martyn and Bethan arrived in Port Talbot, Wales, on February 1, 1927. Martyn began pastoring a small church, the Forward Movement Mission Hall, in Sandfields, at Aberavon.

On October 26, Lloyd-Jones was officially ordained into the ministry as a Calvinistic Methodist. His home church in London was not large enough to house the curious crowd that gathered to see this eminent physician set apart for gospel ministry, so the service was held in George Whitefield's Tabernacle in London.

Humanly speaking, this could not have been a worse time to come to South Wales. Unemployment, drunkenness, and illiteracy were rampant among the townspeople. The Great Depression would hit in 1929. The people were not well educated. Only a small percentage of the local people attended the church, and the previous pastor had left quite discouraged.

Nevertheless, Lloyd-Jones believed they needed to hear straightforward, doctrinal preaching from the Scripture. Such preaching would later be called "logic on fire." He based his pulpit ministry exclusively on the Bible. He never cracked jokes, nor used any kind of anecdotes or personal stories. He was simply consumed with a zeal for the glory of God, and he sought to proclaim it from the Word of God in the power of the Holy Spirit.

By the beginning of his pastorate, the church in Sandfields had shrunk to only ninety-three members. Worse, many in the congregation had become enamored with the social gospel. Lloyd-Jones chose to pursue the old paths of biblical exposition to build the church. The drama society was suspended. Musical evenings were canceled. Gospel preaching was reestablished. And as Lloyd-Jones preached the Word, the church began to grow.

STRAIGHTFORWARD BIBLICAL PREACHING

Immediately, the church came alive. Church members were converted. Even the church secretary was saved. A spiritualist medium came to faith in Christ. Bethan herself was converted to Christ. She testified, "I was for two years under Martyn's ministry before I really understood what the gospel was. . . . I thought you had to be a drunkard or a prostitute to be converted." Only those with a credible profession of Christ were allowed to remain in the church membership. Those empty confessors of Christ were removed from the church roll. In his eleven years at Sandfields, numerous people were converted to Christ and joined the church.

This congregation was transformed by the power of the Word of God delivered by this passionate preacher. Iain Murray describes what took place during these early years of ministry:

He seemed to be exclusively interested in the purely "traditional" part of church life, which consisted of the regular Sunday Services (at 11 a.m. and 6 p.m.), a prayer meeting on Mondays and a mid-week meeting on Wednesdays. Everything else could go, and thus those activities particularly designed to attract the outsiders soon came to an end. The demise of the dramatic society posed a practical problem, namely, what to do with the wooden stage which occupied a part of the church hall? "You can heat the church with it," the new minister told the Committee. . . . The church was to advance, not by approximating to the world, but rather by representing in the world the true life and privilege of the children of God.[8]

GROWING INFLUENCE ABROAD

By the 1930s, Lloyd-Jones' powerful preaching was drawing attention on a wide scale. Invitations took him to conferences around Wales, where thousands came to hear him preach. In one year, he preached in fifty-five meetings away from Sandfields. The secular press was describing him as the most prominent preacher in Wales since the revival of 1904. On one occasion, in 1935, he preached to seven thousand at the Daniel Rowland's Centenary Meeting. On another

---

8. Ibid., 135.

occasion, he returned to London and preached to thousands in the Royal Albert Hall. In 1937, Lloyd-Jones traveled to the United States, where he preached in Pittsburgh, Philadelphia, and New York.

G. Campbell Morgan, the well-known minister of Westminster Chapel, London, was so impressed with Lloyd-Jones that in 1938, he asked him to join the work at Westminster. Lloyd-Jones initially declined because an academic teaching post at his denomination's theological college in Bala, North Wales, had been discussed with him. But due to a strange twist in providence, the position was not offered. In July 1938, he accepted the call to assist Morgan at Westminster Chapel in central London, the largest free church in the city.

To Westminster Chapel

In September 1938, Lloyd-Jones arrived in London to be the assistant to Morgan. At the time, Martyn believed this appointment would only be for six months. However, the pending offer to be the head of another theological school in Wales was not extended to him. It was clear that Lloyd-Jones was to remain in the pulpit.

That same year, he became president of the Inter-Varsity Fellowship of Students. He eventually became copastor with Morgan until, in 1943, the elder preacher retired, leaving Lloyd-Jones to be the sole pastor of Westminster Chapel.

He would fill its pulpit for the next twenty-five years, during which time Westminster Chapel would become a great gospel beacon that shone forth the light of the gospel, resulting in countless lives' being transformed.

By the time World War II ended, most of the members of Westminster Chapel had moved out of London for the safety of the countryside. The membership had dwindled considerably from the pre-war years. There was some question as to whether the congregation could survive if strategies other than Bible preaching were not used. Some in the chapel wanted to add a choir and evening organ recitals to build up attendance. But Lloyd-Jones refused to capitulate. He set his gaze to preach and in time, the first balcony was opened again. Then, the second balcony was reopened. Eventually, the sanctuary was full.

A LONELY VOICE IN ENGLAND

In this hour, Lloyd-Jones preached in such a way that the Word of God greatly stirred the hearts and consciences of his hearers. As he stood in the Westminster pulpit, he modeled an unwavering commitment to the centrality of a biblically centered ministry that desperately needed to be recovered. Despite the opposing drift of society, Lloyd-Jones refused to cave in to the surrounding pressures that clamored for worldly entertainment to attract people. Instead, he relied entirely on the power of God in the preaching of His word. Iain Murray writes:

In the 1950s Martyn Lloyd-Jones was virtually alone
in England in engaging in what he meant by "expository preaching." For preaching to qualify for that
designation it was not enough, in his view, that its
content be biblical; addresses which concentrated
upon word-studies, or which gave running commentary and analyses of whole chapters, might be
termed "biblical," but that is not the same as exposition. To expound is not simply to give the correct
grammatical sense of a verse or passage, it is rather to
set out the principles or doctrines which the words
are intended to convey. True expository preaching is,
therefore, *doctrinal* preaching, it is preaching which
addresses specific truths from God to man. The
expository preacher is not one who "shares his studies" with others, he is an ambassador and a messenger,
authoritatively delivering the Word of God to men.
Such preaching presents a text, then, with that text in
sight throughout, there is deduction, argument and
appeal, the whole making up a message which bears
the authority of Scripture itself.[9]

Lloyd-Jones was the personification of his own definition
of preaching, namely, "theology coming through a man who is
on fire." Preaching, he believed, is "God's method," that is, the

---

9. Murray, *The Fight of Faith*, 261.

primary means by which the truth of Scripture is to be made known. In this way, Lloyd-Jones stood with the Reformers and Puritans, who centuries earlier insisted that preaching is the chief means by which the grace of God is administered to the church.

In October 1954, Lloyd-Jones began his famous, verse-by-verse exposition of the Sermon on the Mount with saving and sanctifying power. That same year, he enthusiastically supported the inaugural Puritan Conference at Westminster Chapel, a gathering that focused upon the Puritan movement. He believed such a resurgence of Puritan convictions was desperately needed again in the sterile churches of England. In 1952, he launched his monumental Friday-evening preaching series that would continue for the next sixteen years until his retirement in 1968. This began with a three-year series on great doctrines of the Bible (1952–55), which would be followed by his thirteen-year-long exposition of Romans (1955–68). From small beginnings in the fellowship hall, the growing numbers forced it to be moved into the sanctuary, where it became a main staple for many eager listeners who devoured every word.

Seeking Revival

The underlying desire of Lloyd-Jones for the church was for a genuine revival, such as had been experienced in the

Evangelical and Great Awakenings of the eighteenth century. He longed for a day when preaching like that of George White-field, Jonathan Edwards, and others would come to England. Consequently, he knew two life-threatening extremes would have to be avoided. On one hand, he wanted to avoid the dead orthodoxy of a cold Calvinism. On the other extreme, he knew the emotional excesses of the Pentecostal and other emotional movements had to be guarded against.

What Lloyd-Jones desired was an experiential Reformed movement. On the centennial anniversary of the Revival of 1859, he preached a series of sermons on revival in which he proclaimed his desire for God to restore the fullness of His power to the church. Only a genuine awakening, he believed, could resuscitate churches that had grown confident in themselves, resulting in worldliness, weak doctrine, and shallow spiritual experience.

Some evidences of a spiritual revival came to Westminster. People were drawn to the chapel from a broad cross-section of life to hear the Word of God. Doctors and nurses from the medical community were found among the congregation. Members of Parliament sat under the preaching. Students from all parts of the world attended. Servants of the royal household came. Beyond the great numbers though, it was what God was doing in the lives of those who came. Countless people were converted. Students were called into ministry and the mission field. There is no explanation for what occurred apart from the presence and power of God.

The remainder of the 1950s for Lloyd-Jones proved to be more of the same, year after year, as he saw the divine hand of blessing upon his labor. He remained a fixture in the pulpit and would not be moved. On Sunday mornings, he preached on experiential Christianity for believers. On Sunday evenings, he gave evangelistic messages for the unconverted. On Friday night, he taught doctrinal messages in systematic theology and Romans. Beyond Westminster, he served as a pastor to other pastors by presiding over numerous ministerial fraternals and conferences. In addition, he helped establish the Banner of Truth Trust, which began republishing Puritan classics and other Reformed works.

The 1960s would prove to be the hardest decade in the Doctor's ministry. He would face challenges on several fronts, some involving men with whom he had much in common. First, he feared the spiritual conditions in Britain were worsening and demanded much more attention than he had previously thought. Second, many men who were a part of the doctrinal recovery of the 1950s were now slipping into the modern thinking that these same Reformed truths were too exclusive. He observed the onslaught of ecumenical thought then circulating around Britain. The 1960s were flooded with books, articles, lectures, and conferences in favor of transforming the existing denominations. Many evangelicals, like Lloyd-Jones, had ministered within their various denominations even when those denominations accepted liberal ministers and their original orthodox statements of faith were no longer deemed acceptable. The ecumenical movement in Britain during this time comprised those denominations that urged everyone to come together as "one church" by 1980.[10] This movement caused evangelicals to carefully consider a proper response.

TRUE ECUMENISM

For Lloyd-Jones, the real issue was the need for a proper definition of who a Christian is, an understanding of how we receive forgiveness of sins, and a doctrine of what makes a church.[11] There were some evangelical leaders, including J.I. Packer and John Stott, who wanted to work within their denominations to be an evangelical voice and influence, while other evangelical ministers had already left their denominations to found independent churches. Philip H. Eveson, former minister of Kensit Evangelical Church in London, said, "Lloyd-Jones found it inconsistent that those evangelicals attached to doctrinally mixed denominations were happy to work together with other evangelicals from differing denominational backgrounds in evangelical parachurch organizations, but were not interested in being more together as churches."[12] Lloyd-Jones was most interested in a loose kind of association of evangelical denominations and churches over against the liberal kind of ecumenism.

Lloyd-Jones believed this ecumenical movement was

---

10. Eveson, personal correspondence with the author.
11. Iain H. Murray, *Evangelicalism Divided* (Edinburgh, Scotland: Banner of Truth, 2001), 48.
12. Ibid.

threatening the very life of the churches. This subject was the topic of two addresses which he gave to the Westminster Fellowship in Welwyn in the summer of 1962. In his expositions of John 17 and Ephesians 4, he showed the biblical definition of what it means to be a Christian and how this must precede an understanding of Christian unity. He pointed out that in the term *Christian*, there is the necessity for both orthodox belief and personal experience. True Christians are those who have confessed and repented of their sin, embraced Christ as their only hope, and now possess a new life because of a new birth. These timely addresses were published by the IVP in December 1962 under the title *The Basis of Christian Unity*.[13]

In response, many ecumenists criticized Lloyd-Jones. From major universities and prominent pulpits in England, Lloyd-Jones was openly assaulted. However, this type of criticism did not deter Lloyd-Jones from addressing the shift in British evangelicalism. The ecumenical movement had raised some serious questions that would have to be properly addressed doctrinally. The Doctor believed this crisis presented a unique opportunity to speak to what constitutes true unity. He lamented that doctrinal commitment was weakening among many evangelicals in order to achieve wider success and influence. In fact, he had witnessed this earlier in the wider position Billy Graham had assumed in the 1950s. Graham became well known in England during his crusade in Harringay Arena in 1954.

---

13. Reprinted in Martyn Lloyd-Jones, *Knowing the Times* (Edinburgh, Scotland: Banner of Truth, 1989), 118–63.

In 1963, Lloyd-Jones and Graham asked Lloyd-Jones to chair the World Congress on Evangelism that was to take place in Europe. Meeting in the vestry of Westminster Chapel in July 1963, Lloyd-Jones expressed to Graham that he would be very happy to chair the upcoming World Congress on Evangelism if Graham would cease the general sponsorship of his campaigns, forfeit his involvement with liberals and Roman Catholics, and drop the invitation system at the end of the sermon.[14] The American evangelist could not meet these conditions, instead calling for a "new day of understanding and dialogue."[15] Graham would later go on to participate in ministry involvement with those leading the ecumenical movement in Europe. This was unacceptable for Lloyd-Jones, and he declined Graham's invitation.

By the end of 1965, the lines of division were clearly drawn. Lloyd-Jones wrote to Philip Hughes in the United States, "I am sure that we are heading up during this next year to a real crisis."[16] Lloyd-Jones was calling for a new, visible group of evangelicals and introduced the idea of schism if those in the ecumenical movement did not cooperate. In essence, this made unity something other than just spiritual. Lloyd-Jones believed that the way to lasting cooperation was

---

14. Iain H. Murray, *The Life of Martyn Lloyd-Jones, 1899–1981* (Edinburgh, Scotland: Banner of Truth, 2013), 371.

15. Ibid.

16. Letter of December 12, 1965, *D. Martyn Lloyd-Jones: Letters, 1919–1981* (Edinburgh, Scotland: Banner of Truth, 1994), 167.

for churches and preachers alike to wholeheartedly submit themselves to the authority of Scripture on all the essential doctrines of the Christian faith.

In October 1966, the controversy became public. At the second assembly of the National Association of Evangelicals, Lloyd-Jones became entangled in a public confrontation that divided the evangelical movement. In his address, he called for a wide expression of unity by the formation of a federation of evangelical churches that held orthodox convictions. His desire was for a "fellowship or an association of evangelical churches." John Stott, rector of All Souls Church, London, was the chairman of the meeting and responded by rejecting this plea for a new association. He feared that ministers would leave their denominations, including the Church of England, of which he was a part. The inevitable result was separation. Eventually, for this and other reasons, the Puritan Conference was canceled and the Westminster Conference was founded for ministers who held a stricter allegiance to the Word of God.

Retired from Westminster

In 1968, the preaching ministry of Lloyd-Jones at Westminster Chapel came to an unexpected end when he was found to have colon cancer. On March 1, Lloyd-Jones preached his last sermon at the chapel, and the following Thursday, he underwent successful surgery. But rather than return to the chapel, Lloyd-Jones announced his retirement and stepped down without allowing any ceremonial farewell. He withdrew into a ministry of writing and itinerant preaching, where his influence would be more widespread. He spent much of his time editing his sermon transcripts for publication, the most significant being his Friday-night sermons on Romans. Through the printed page, his pulpit ministry shaped a new generation of preachers and believers. He also spoke occasionally on British television and radio. Moreover, as he had done for several years, he accepted preaching invitations throughout the country and abroad. Many of these assignments were taken in order to encourage young ministers in their pastorates. One significant trip took him to Westminster Theological Seminary in Philadelphia, where he gave sixteen lectures on preaching that became his classic book, *Preaching and Preachers*. Through these messages put into print, he has influenced countless preachers in expository preaching.

FAITHFUL TO THE END

Lloyd-Jones preached what would be his last sermon at Barcombe Baptist Church on June 8, 1980. Two days before his death, in 1981, he wrote with a trembling hand a note to his wife and children: "Do not pray for healing. Do not hold me back from the glory."[17] The next Sunday, on March 1, exactly thirteen years to the day after he preached his last sermon at Westminster, he died peacefully in his sleep and entered into glory to meet the God whom he so cherished. John Stott said, "The most powerful and persuasive voice in Britain for some thirty years is now silent."[18] Lloyd-Jones had been a student of church history, and among his most treasured thoughts was a statement by John Wesley, who said of the early Methodists, "Our people die well." In his own death, he knew the blessed reality of those words.

Lloyd-Jones was buried at Newcastle Emlyn, near Cardigan, west Wales. This burial place was personally selected by Lloyd-Jones not only because of a personal connection with his own family and his childhood, but also because of his great affection for his wife, Bethan, whose family was buried there.

In this Welsh graveyard lies a simple tomb. On it are inscribed the words of the biblical text that he preached in his first sermon at Aberavon fifty-five years earlier:

Martyn Lloyd-Jones 1899–1981

"For I determined not to know anything among you save Jesus Christ and Him crucified."

17. Michael Rusten and Sharon O. Rusten, *The One Year Christian History* (Wheaton, Ill.: Tyndale House, 2003), 115.
18. Back cover of Murray, *The Life of Martyn Lloyd-Jones*.

Written by the Apostle Paul, this inspired verse, 1 Corinthians 2:2, is a fitting summary of the life and ministry of Lloyd-Jones. He was one who had resolved to proclaim the person and work of Jesus Christ. To this calling, he remained true until his death.

CHAPTER TWO

Sovereignly Called

Martyn Lloyd-Jones combined Calvin's love for truth and sound Reformed doctrine with the fire and passion of the eighteenth-century Methodist revival. . . . He was by God's grace and gifting, a great preacher.[1]

—JOHN PIPER

Martyn Lloyd-Jones was many things. He was a noted author, evangelical leader, conference convener, founding publisher, and much more. But first and foremost, Lloyd-Jones was a preacher—an *expository* preacher. In an hour when the authoritative voice in the British pulpit had grown silent, God raised up this fiery Welshman to restore it to its former glory as during the sixteenth- and seventeenth-century Puritan Age and the eighteenth-century Evangelical

---

1. John Piper, "Martyn Lloyd-Jones: The Preacher," in *Preaching and Preachers: 40th Anniversary Edition,* by D. Martyn Lloyd-Jones (Grand Rapids, Mich.: Zondervan, 2009), 153.

Awakening. The Doctor believed a cold professionalism and sterile academicism had crept into the modern-day pulpit. Lloyd-Jones ignited a fire in the pulpit that rekindled biblical preaching in the twentieth century that has spread to this present hour.

By any human estimate, though, the last man anyone would have suspected to be called to such a mission was this young, aspiring physician. By his mid-twenties, Lloyd-Jones had embarked upon a career path that was launching him to the pinnacle of the medical profession. He had within his grasp virtually everything the world had to offer. He was well-positioned to ascend to the summit of his chosen field. Yet unknown to the world and to Lloyd-Jones himself, God had chosen an entirely different path for this medical doctor. The invisible hand of providence was directing him to another call.

Lloyd-Jones would no longer be used for the care of the body, but for the healing of the soul. He was the unsuspecting recipient of the heavenly call to preach the Word. The Scripture teaches not many of the mighty or noble are chosen by God for salvation or for His service. For the most part, it was ordinary men—fishermen, tax collectors, and the like—whom the Lord called. There are, however, some men whom God calls who are rising to the top rung of the world's ladder of success. Some are men like Luke and Paul, well educated and cultured. This was certainly the case with this brilliant clinician, Martyn Lloyd-Jones.

As a young physician, Lloyd-Jones came to the realization

that in his medical practice, he was helping his patients to recover physically only to return to a decadent life spiritually. Martyn recognized that he was merely attending to their superficial needs, but not addressing their deepest need regarding their relationship with God. Lloyd-Jones realized he must give himself to the healing of the soul rather than the body.

An Intense Inner Struggle

At the age of twenty-six, the Doctor became embroiled in an intense struggle over the call of God upon his life. He was so consumed with ascertaining the divine direction that it adversely affected his physical health, as he lost some twenty pounds from his already thin frame. In this search for the will of God, there was no rest for his troubled soul nor sleep for his weakening body. In this crisis, Lloyd-Jones wrestled with God like Jacob with the angel of the Lord, to discern God's path. In this travail, he realized that God was calling him into the ministry.

This desperate search reached its zenith one night when he, Bethan, and another couple went to a theater in Leicester Square, London. When the play was over, the four of them exited the theater and walked out into the bright lights of the busy square. There, Lloyd-Jones observed a Salvation Army band playing hymns and giving a gospel witness. He was immediately struck by their strong convictions in the Lord. As he witnessed this little ministry team proclaiming the message of salvation, he concluded in that decisive moment, "These are my people."[2] In that pivotal event he crossed the line and answered God's call upon his life to preach the Word. Reflecting upon this time, Lloyd-Jones summarized it this way:

> I have never forgotten it. There is a theme in Wagner's opera *Tannhäuser*, the two pulls—the pull of the world and the chorus of the pilgrims—and the contrast between the two. I have very often thought of it. I know exactly what it means. I suppose I had enjoyed the play. When I heard this band and the hymns I said, "These are my people, these are the people I belong to, and I am going to belong to them."[3]

Surrendering to the call of God, Lloyd-Jones walked away from a life in medicine in order to preach the gospel. He gave himself entirely to the ministry in order to proclaim the unsearchable riches of Christ and to follow the will of God wherever it led.

A Shocking Effect

As the news of this decision swept through the medical community, it spread like wildfire. People asked why he would

---

2. Ibid., 93.
3. Ibid.

give up such a promising career in medicine. Observers reasoned if he had been a bookie and wanted to give up that kind of work to preach the gospel, it would be understandable. But who would leave the practice of medicine—a good profession that helps people—in order to be one more minister in a dying church?

To these skeptics and critics, Lloyd-Jones replied that if they knew the power of the gospel, they would not respond as they did:

> "Ah well!" I felt like saying to them, "if you knew more about the work of a doctor you would understand. We but spend most of our time rendering people fit to go back to their sin!" . . . I saw I was helping these men to sin and I decided that I would do no more of it. I want to heal souls. If a man has a diseased body and his soul is all right, he is all right to the end but a man with a healthy body and a diseased soul is all right for sixty years or so and then he has to face an eternity of hell. Ah, yes! We have sometimes to give up those things which are good for that which is the best of all.[4]

In reality, Lloyd-Jones gave up what was good in order to pursue what was better—in fact, what was best. Upon leaving the medical profession, the Doctor frankly said: "I gave up nothing; I received everything. I count it the highest honor

---

4. Murray, *The First Forty Years*, 80.

that God can confer on any man to call him to be a herald of the gospel."[5] To him, the pulpit where the preacher stood was sacred ground, uniquely set apart by God. In his mind, he gave up the temporal for the eternal, the human for the divine, the earthly for the heavenly. This was not a sacrifice, but a promotion.

By divine initiative, Lloyd-Jones understood that God had sought him for this lofty call to preach. He believed this was a calling so holy that no man may assume it for himself. God Himself must lay this charge at a man's feet. In Lloyd-Jones' mind, preaching is a divine assignment that can only be issued by God. The Doctor asserted, "A preacher is not a Christian who decides to preach, he does not just decide to do it; he does not even decide to take up preaching as a calling."[6] This is to say, such a decision must never originate with any man, but come down from above. He maintained, "It is God who commands preaching, it is God who sends out preachers."[7] It was in obedience to this divine command that this young physician dedicated his life to preaching.

Lloyd-Jones was convinced that such a call to the ministry is thrust upon a man. It is God who acts upon the heart. Such a heavenly calling originates with God, not man. Lloyd-Jones addressed this divine source of the call when he explained:

---

5. Lloyd-Jones, *Preaching and Preachers*, 9.

6. Ibid., 103.

7. Murray, *The First Forty Years*, 80.

Am I called to be a preacher or not? How do you know? . . . This is something that happens to you; it is God dealing with you, and God acting upon you by His Spirit; it is something you become aware of rather than what you do. It is thrust upon you, it is presented to you and almost forced upon you constantly in this way.[8]

What a Man Must Do

If there is anything else a man can do other than preach, Lloyd-Jones maintained, he ought to do it. The pulpit is no place for him. The ministry is not merely something an individual *can* do, but what he *must* do. To enter the pulpit, that necessity must be laid upon him. A God-called man, he believed, would rather die than live without preaching. Lloyd-Jones often quoted the famed British pastor Charles H. Spurgeon: "If you can do anything else do it. If you can stay out of the ministry, stay out of the ministry."[9] In other words, only those who believe they are chosen by God for the pulpit should proceed in undertaking this sacred task.

"Preachers are born, not made," Lloyd-Jones asserted. "This is an absolute. You will never teach a man to be a preacher if he is not already one."[10] It was clearly the case in

---

8. Lloyd-Jones, *Preaching and Preachers*, 104–5.
9. Ibid., 105.
10. Ibid., 119.

the life of Lloyd-Jones. He realized he was not joining a volunteer army.

What constitutes this call to preach? Lloyd-Jones identified six distinguishing marks of this divine summons to the pulpit. He himself had felt the gravity of each of these realities weighing heavily upon his own soul. He believed the same spiritual forces should come to bear on all preachers.

First, Lloyd-Jones affirmed there must be an *inner compulsion* within the one called to preach the Word. He stated there must be "a consciousness within one's own spirit, an awareness of a kind of pressure being brought to bear upon one's spirit."[11] He identified this as an irresistible impulse, as "some disturbance in the realm of the spirit" that "your mind is directed to the whole question of preaching."[12] This inner coercion becomes "the most dominant force in their lives."[13] Lloyd-Jones explained, "This is something that happens to you, and God acting upon you by His Spirit, it is something you become aware of rather than what you do."[14] In other words, the drive to preach becomes a burden upon the heart that must be fulfilled. It is a holy preoccupation within the soul that causes the one called to step out in faith and embrace the work.

This divine calling, Lloyd-Jones believed, grips the soul and governs the spirit. It becomes an overwhelming obsession

---

11. Ibid., 104.
12. Ibid.
13. Ibid.
14. Ibid.

that cannot be discarded. It will not go away nor leave a man to himself. He explained that there becomes no way of escape. Such a strong force lays hold of the man that he is held captive. Lloyd-Jones recognizes this when he states:

> You do your utmost to push back and to rid yourself of this disturbance in your spirit which comes in these various ways. But you reach the point when you cannot do so any longer. It almost becomes an obsession, and so overwhelming that in the end you say, "I can do nothing else, I cannot resist any longer."[15]

Second, Lloyd-Jones emphasized there will be an *outside influence* that will come to the one called. The input and counsel of other believers becomes influential to the one destined for the ministry. It may be the feedback of a pastor or the affirmation of an elder. It could be the encouragement of another believer. When they hear this person speak the Word, perhaps in a class or Bible study, they are often the best discerners of the man who is called into the ministry. In other words, observant people often recognize the hand of God upon that person before he senses it. Those who best know God and most love His Word often can detect who is being set apart for this work. They give insightful affirmation to the individual being called.

---

15. Ibid., 105–6.

Third, Lloyd-Jones asserted the one called will experience a *loving concern* for others. God gives to the one chosen to preach an overwhelming compassion for the people. As part of this divine choice, the Holy Spirit imparts a consuming desire for the spiritual welfare of others. Lloyd-Jones wrote: "The true call always includes a concern about others, an interest in them, a realization of their lost estate and condition, and a desire to do something about them, and to tell them the message and point them to the way of salvation."[16] This love for others includes the distinct realization that countless people are perishing without Christ. What is more, there is a concern that many of these lost souls are in the church. The one called to preach feels compelled to awaken them to their need for Christ. He is constrained to reach them with the saving message of the gospel.

In Lloyd-Jones' life, he experienced this growing concern for others. He said, "I used to be struck almost dumb sometimes in London at night when I stood watching the cars passing, taking people to the theatres and other places with all their talk and excitement, as I suddenly realized that what all this meant was that these people were looking for peace, peace from themselves."[17] His growing concern was now not for their physical health, but for their spiritual welfare.

Fourth, Lloyd-Jones affirmed there is an *overwhelming constraint* within the one called to do this work. He

---

16. Ibid., 104–5.
17. Murray, *The First Forty Years*, 94–95.

maintained there will be "a sense of constraint,"[18] meaning he feels hemmed in to do this work. It is as though God will not let him be released from his duty to preach. There is nothing else he can do but pursue this inner drive to preach. Necessity is laid upon him, and he *must* preach regardless of what others may say. He *must* minister the Word, no matter what obstacles must be overcome.

Fifth, Lloyd-Jones believed the man who is called to preach comes under a *sobering humility*. He believed that this person is overwhelmed with a deep sense of his own personal unworthiness for such a high and holy task and is often hesitant to move forward to preach for fear of his own inadequacies. Lloyd-Jones writes, "The man who is called by God is a man who realizes what he is called to do, and he so realizes the awfulness of the task that he shrinks from it."[19] Though he is compelled to preach, he is at the same time fearful of doing so. He is sobered by this weighty assignment to speak on behalf of God. He trembles at this stewardship entrusted to him and the accountability that comes with it.

Sixth, Lloyd-Jones added that a *corporate confirmation* must come to the one called to preach. The man who is chosen by God to preach, he argued, must be observed and tested by others in the church. Only then may he be sent from the church. Lloyd-Jones reasoned from Romans 10:13–15 that preachers are "sent," which he understands to mean a formal

---

18. Lloyd-Jones, *Preaching and Preachers*, 105.
19. Ibid., 107.

commissioning by a sending church. The leaders of the church must examine the qualifications of the one set apart to preach and affirm the validity of this call. Hands must be laid upon him in recognition of what God is doing in his life.

According to Lloyd-Jones, these are the distinguishing marks of a call to gospel ministry. To one extent or another, each of these six realities must be present in the life of one who has been set apart by God to preach. Each of these factors is necessary in order to ascertain one's call to preach. Lloyd-Jones had experienced each one of these in his life. Further, he encouraged others to discern the presence of these hallmarks in their lives.

SOME IMPORTANT IMPLICATIONS

Because these marks must be found in a God-called man, Lloyd-Jones further reasoned that two implications are necessarily true. Given the factors previously stated, these are reasonable deductions to be drawn.

The first implication concerns the matter of *theological training*. Lloyd-Jones believed that no seminary can make a preacher. Only God can do so. As a result, he chose not to attend a theological school. He was convinced that God had called and gifted him to preach. He believed through his own personal reading and strenuous study that he was fit for the task to which he was called. He also refused honorary doctorates. In keeping with this, he believed no man should go to an institution of higher theological training in order to be made a preacher.

After his retirement, Lloyd-Jones founded the London Theological Seminary with the intent of training men for the ministry. But unlike other theological schools, he determined that there would be no awarding of diplomas and degrees. He believed that the awarding of degrees would give a false perception that a man is now made a preacher. However, if a man is genuinely gifted by God to be a preacher, a theological school can enhance and develop what God has already given him. This ministerial training can only improve a man to a limited extent. It is the divine call that supplies what is most essential.

The second implication concerns the ministry of *lay preachers*. With the dearth of true Bible preachers in England, a movement of lay preachers had emerged during the days of Lloyd-Jones to fill this shortage. Lloyd-Jones saw this not as a solution, but as exchanging one problem for another. He rejected the legitimacy of lay preachers because he believed not all believers are chosen to preach. Only those called to the pulpit should preach, and no others should be allowed to do so. He certainly affirmed that every Christian is commanded by God to be His witness. But only those called to preach should be permitted to step into the pulpit to expound the Scripture. All Christians are to share the gospel, but only those called to preach are to fulfill this high calling in the church.

More preachers was not the answer to the dilemma of a shortage of preachers. Rather, the solution called for recognizing and training the preachers who have been gifted by God to preach—even if that meant fewer preachers.

THE HIGHEST, GREATEST CALL

In 1969, after his pastoral retirement, Lloyd-Jones gave a series of lectures on the subject of preaching at Westminster Theological Seminary in Philadelphia. In these addresses, he began by elevating the high call to preach the Word. He said:

> The work of preaching is the highest and the greatest and the most glorious calling to which anyone can ever be called. If you want something in addition to that I would say without any hesitation that the most urgent need in the Christian Church today is true preaching; and as it is the greatest and most urgent need in the Church, it is obviously the greatest need of the world also.[20]

By these words, Lloyd-Jones affirmed that preaching is a sacred call to the office of the preacher. In fact, the highest call under heaven, he believed, is to be a preacher of the inspired Word. It is God who determines the path that our lives take, and not we ourselves. We are not, as the Doctor liked to remind his listeners, "the master of our fate." That attitude

---

20. Ibid., 9.

belongs to the humanist arrogance of a Victorian poem, not the wisdom of God.

As a result, the preacher must be given wholeheartedly to this demanding task. Lloyd-Jones explains: "The preacher is a man of one thing. This is the thing to which he is called, and it is the great passion of his life."[21] The one called must be singularly focused upon this divine charge. This constraining summons to preach must be the driving force of a man's ministry. To this holy call Lloyd-Jones gave himself with the utmost devotion.

---

21. Ibid., 166.

CHAPTER THREE

Biblically Based

Martyn Lloyd-Jones was to twentieth-century England what Charles Spurgeon was to nineteenth century England. The very mention of Lloyd-Jones' name among evangelicals brings to mind a man deeply committed to verse-by-verse preaching of the Word of God with a pathos that is rare in the history of the church.[1]

—R.C. SPROUL

Into the dense darkness of twentieth-century England, the preaching of Martyn Lloyd-Jones shone brightly. The fiery Welsh-born preacher ministered in an hour that had witnessed "the decline in powerful biblical preaching in the English-speaking world."[2] The church, he maintained, had forfeited its once-lofty commitment to the authority of

---

1. Back cover of *The Chirst-Centered Preaching of Martyn Lloyd-Jones.*
2. Alexander, foreword to *The Cross,* viii.

Scripture and exchanged it for the bankruptcy of man's own empty musings. He warned, "Men's opinions have taken the place of God's truth, and the people in their need are turning to the cults, and are listening to any false authority that offers itself to them."[3] It was in such a decadent day that Lloyd-Jones ascended the Westminster Chapel pulpit.

Despite the many compromises that confronted him, Lloyd-Jones staunchly refused to cave in to the pressures to become a "modern man." He was, in reality, a Puritan born out of time, who staunchly resisted the clamoring for man-centered attractions. He refused to embrace the church growth techniques that were becoming popular with many churches. Instead, Lloyd-Jones relied upon the exposition of the Word to build the church. Inheriting a low of 150 attendees at the chapel during World War II, he eventually preached to full-capacity crowds of 2,500 worshipers on Sunday mornings and evenings and 1,200 people each Friday evening. But more important than increased numbers was the fact that people were being converted and transformed into the image of Christ.

Throughout his ministry, Lloyd-Jones insisted that preaching the Bible must always be the first priority in the church. In spite of his many skeptics, he chose to give himself to expository preaching in a day when it had become a lost art. He reintroduced sequential, verse-by-verse preaching to a new generation. In this approach, Hughes Oliphant Old insists, Lloyd-Jones

---

3. D. Martyn Lloyd-Jones, *The Christian Soldier: An Exposition of Ephesians 6:10–20* (Grand Rapids, Mich.: Baker, 1977), 211.

was "breathing new life into a very classic form."[4] He was able to "recover and popularize" expository preaching "throughout the English-speaking world."[5] He launched this resurgence in biblical exposition at a time when "classic expository preaching . . . had all but died out."[6] The return to expository preaching that we see in many places finds its beginnings here.

Resisting contemporary trends, Lloyd-Jones riveted his focus upon the biblical text with an unwavering devotion uncommon in his day. He insisted, "The message should always arise out of the Scriptures directly."[7] In other words, the sermon must begin with a specific text of Scripture and stay with it throughout the message. He maintained, "It is always good to start with a text."[8] The sermon must say what the text says, not what the preacher wants the text to say. The preacher should simply be a mouthpiece for the God-inspired text, nothing more. To this end, Lloyd-Jones asserted: "It should be clear to people that what we are saying is something that comes out of the Bible. We are presenting the Bible and its message. That is the origin of our message."[9] Simply put, true preaching "must always be expository."[10]

---

4. Hughes Oliphant Old, *The Reading and Preaching of the Scriptures in the Worship of the Christian Church, Vol. 6: The Modern Age* (Grand Rapids, Mich.: Eerdmans, 2007), 946.

5. Ibid.

6. Ibid.

7. Lloyd-Jones, *Preaching and Preachers: 40th Anniversary Edition*, 201.

8. D. Martyn Lloyd-Jones, *Great Doctrines of the Bible* (Wheaton, Ill.: Crossway, 2003), 1.

9. Lloyd-Jones, *Preaching and Preachers*, 75.

10. Ibid.

PUTTING NEW LIFE INTO AN OLD FORM

Lloyd-Jones is best known for his disciplined approach to preaching, which largely involved long, protracted series through entire chapters or books of the Bible. Throughout his ministry, he most often followed the *lectio continua* approach, meaning "continuous expositions." He believed that with this verse-by-verse preaching style, he most consistently served a balanced diet to his well-fed congregation.

With this intensely biblical focus, Lloyd-Jones delivered more than four thousand sermons from his Westminster Chapel pulpit during his thirty-year pastorate there. From 1938 to 1968, he usually preached twice on Sundays—once in the morning and once in the evening. In addition, beginning in 1952, he also preached on Friday evenings until he retired in 1968. For these sixteen years, he preached on Friday night every September to May. During the week, he also conducted regular preaching tours throughout the English countryside. In these travels, he often preached multiple times in addition to his Westminster duties. Moreover, he preached in many conferences in England and Wales. Added to this were occasional preaching responsibilities at numerous pastors' conferences in the United States, where he was becoming as well known as he was in England.

In his preaching, Lloyd-Jones was singularly committed to expounding the Word of God. This discipline was based upon his fundamental belief in the Bible itself. He was convinced that Scripture is what it claims to be—divinely inspired and supremely authoritative. He believed that when the Bible speaks, God speaks. Therefore, he was determined to preach the Bible's truths with unwavering resilience. The supernatural nature of the Bible, he believed, *mandated* expository preaching.

More specifically, what did Lloyd-Jones say regarding the many perfections of the Word of God? In what follows, the focus will be upon his understanding of two of these perfections: the divine inspiration and supreme authority of Scripture.

THE GOD-BREATHED WORD

With unshakable certainty, Lloyd-Jones asserted that "the Scriptures are a divine product breathed out by God."[11] Scripture's human authors were the chosen instruments used by God to write His divine Word. These men were merely the secondary authors of the Bible, tools in the hand of God. There was only one primary Author, namely, God Himself. The Scriptures, he maintained, "were produced by the creative breath of the almighty God."[12] From cover to cover, the entire Bible is the written Word of God, not the word of men.

Lloyd-Jones believed in the inspiration of Scripture in a specific way. He affirmed the *verbal* inspiration of the Bible. That is, he maintained that every word of the Bible is the

11. Lloyd-Jones, *Great Doctrines*, 24.
12. Ibid.

infallible product of God Himself. When Lloyd-Jones asserted the divine inspiration of Scripture, he believed it is breathed out of the mouth of God. He stated:

> Inspired really means "God-breathed." We mean that God breathed these messages into men and through them, and these Scriptures are the result of that divine action. We believe that they were produced by the creative breath of the almighty God. Put in a simpler form, we mean that everything we have here has been given by God to man.[13]

Lloyd-Jones did not believe that the Bible merely contains general thoughts and vague ideas from God. To the contrary, he asserted, "It is not merely that the thoughts are inspired, not merely the idea." He contended that the doctrine of inspiration extends to "the actual record, down to the particular words."[14] With this confession, Lloyd-Jones affirmed the full inspiration of every word of Scripture. He stated: "The Bible claims for itself what is called *verbal inspiration*. It is not merely that the thoughts are inspired, not merely the ideas, but the actual record, down to the particular words. It is not merely that the statements are correct, but that every word is divinely inspired."[15] Such precision influenced his search

---

13. Ibid.
14. Ibid.
15. Ibid., 24.

for the God-intended interpretation of the Word and the certainty with which he preached it.

In the recording of Scripture, Lloyd-Jones stated, "The Holy Spirit has thus overruled and controlled and guided these men, even in the particular words, in such a way as to prevent any error, and above all to produce the result that was originally intended by God."[16] Each man wrote his portion of Scripture while using his own vocabulary and peculiar personality with his unique manner of expression. Nevertheless, every recorded word of the Bible is the absolute truth of God. With deep conviction, Lloyd-Jones insisted that the words of Scripture are the very breath of God. Thus, Scripture speaks with the peerless accuracy of God Himself.

ABANDONMENT AND APOSTASY

It was the abandonment of the divine inspiration of Scripture, Lloyd-Jones believed, that was the primary cause for the departure from expository preaching. This, in turn, contributed to the declining power and influence of the church. He maintained, "For me the real cause of the present state of the Church of God on earth is to be found in the Church's voluntary departure from a belief in the Bible as the fully inspired Word of God, and from stressing and emphasizing real evangelical truth."[17] He contended that the elevation of human

---

16. Ibid.
17. D. Martyn Lloyd-Jones, "The Return to the Bible," *Eusebeia* 7 (Spring 2007): 7.

reasoning over divine revelation was the chief reason for the dying state of the church. Lloyd-Jones explained, "From the moment that philosophy was given the place of revelation in our studies and in our pulpits, things really began to go wrong."[18] The church had gone from bad to worse.

Despite the prevalent unbelief in the Bible, Lloyd-Jones noted that people continued to attend church out of a sense of tradition. Initially, it was difficult to see the effect of the change in attitude toward Scripture. People were still in church, and religious activity was being conducted. But the wholesale departure from a fundamental belief in the divine inspiration of Scripture meant the sudden loss of the power of God in preaching. He observed: "Of course, for a time, people continued to attend church and chapel in fairly large numbers, partly out of mere habit and custom, without realizing exactly what was happening."[19] When the church's confidence in the Word departed, the glory of God likewise departed from the church.

Lloyd-Jones claimed, "We can be perfectly certain that the Church lost her authority and power from the moment she ceased to firmly believe in the authority of the Word of God."[20] Such apostasy in the church always leads to its spiritual impotence at every level. This was especially true in the church's witness to the world. Lloyd-Jones concluded that as a

18. Ibid.
19. Ibid.
20. Ibid.

result of the undermining of the authority of the Bible, many churches had lost their evangelistic power. Rather than confronting the world with its sin and preaching the gospel, the church chose to become like the world. With the power of Scripture removed, the church became a social club of unconverted, outwardly religious people.

Addressing the church's unbelief in the divine inspiration of Scripture, Lloyd-Jones pointedly asserted:

> From the moment that the idea began to gain currency that the Bible was the history of the quest of mankind for God, rather than God's revelation of Himself and the only way of salvation to mankind, the Church began to decline and to wane in her influence and in her power. From the time the Church threw overboard the great evangelical doctrines, and substituted for them a belief in the moral and spiritual evolution of mankind, and began to preach a social gospel rather than a personal salvation—from that moment church attendance really became a mere matter of form, or a merely pleasant way of gratifying one's appetite for ceremony, ritual, oratory, and music.[21]

Abandoning Scripture as divinely authored is a point of departure from which the church rarely returns. Nevertheless,

---

21. Ibid., 8.

in his day, Lloyd-Jones stood immovable upon this impregnable rock of the divine inspiration of Scripture. Therefore, he saw himself as a messenger who had been entrusted with a message from God. Further, the entirety of his ministry was to be nothing more than a mouthpiece for the God-breathed Word.

STANDING UPON BIBLICAL AUTHORITY

Given this commitment to divine inspiration, Lloyd-Jones also believed the Scripture speaks with the very authority of God Himself. He did not hesitate to affirm the importance of its right to rule human lives: "This subject of authority is indeed the great theme of the Bible itself. The Bible presents itself to us as an authoritative book."[22] This is to say, Scripture is to be recognized as the highest arbiter and final judge on every matter. There is no higher court of appeal than the Bible. Lloyd-Jones adds, "The authority of the Scriptures is not a matter to be defended, so much as to be asserted. . . . It is the preaching and exposition of the Bible that really establish its truth and authority."[23] By this assertion, he maintained that there is no higher authority in the church than the Word of God.

This truth should have a great effect upon the pulpit. It means that biblical preaching comes with the binding authority of God. To the extent that the pulpit rightly expounds the

22. D. Martyn Lloyd-Jones, *Authority* (1958; repr., Edinburgh, Scotland: Banner of Truth, 1984), 10.
23. Ibid., 41.

Word of God, it comes with commanding power. Lloyd-Jones asserted, "The Scriptures *themselves* claim that authority." He added, "They come to us as the Word of God. . . . You cannot read the Old Testament without feeling that everywhere there is the assumption that this is the Word of God."[24] The preacher who casts doubt upon the Scripture registers a denial of the veracity of God.

For Lloyd-Jones, the supreme authority of Scripture was not a matter of secondary importance. Rather, it was a fundamental matter of first importance in the Christian faith. Everything the church believes and its pulpit proclaims rests squarely upon this chief cornerstone. Either the entire Bible is true and authoritative, he reasoned, or it is to be utterly rejected in whole. For the Doctor, there is no middle ground regarding the Scripture. He stated:

> We all therefore have to face this ultimate and final question: Do we accept the Bible as the Word of God, as the sole authority in all matters of faith and practice, or do we not? Is the whole of my thinking governed by Scripture, or do I come with my reason and pick and choose out of Scripture and sit in judgment upon it, putting myself and modern knowledge forward as the ultimate standard and authority? The issue is crystal clear. Do I accept Scripture as a revelation from

24. Ibid., 50.

God, or do I trust to speculation, human knowledge, human learning, human understanding and human reasons Or, putting it still more simply, Do I pin my faith to, and subject all my thinking to, what I read in the Bible? Or do I defer to modern knowledge, to modern learning, to what people think today, to what we know at this present time which was not known in the past? It is inevitable that we occupy one or the other of those two positions.[25]

These words by Lloyd-Jones should not be passed over lightly. By them, he lays down a challenge before every preacher.

CHRIST, THE APOSTLES, AND BIBLICAL AUTHORITY

Lloyd-Jones' confidence in the authority of Scripture was fortified by the fact that Jesus Christ affirmed its full authority. He believed every preacher must stand where Christ stood on this issue or stand contrary to and against Christ. For Lloyd-Jones, this was fundamentally a matter of submission to the lordship of Christ. He exclaimed, "Our Lord Himself fully accepted that position. How often does He say, 'It is written'! And He directs men to that as the final authority. He meets the attack of Satan by quoting Scripture."[26] When the Scrip-

---

25. Lloyd-Jones, *The Christian Soldier*, 211.
26. Lloyd-Jones, *Authority*, 51.

ture is accepted as authoritative, as based upon the reliable testimony of Christ, the preacher exposits the Scripture with power in the pulpit.

To this point, Lloyd-Jones stressed that Christ affirmed the supreme authority of the Old Testament. With astute insight, he noted, "To the Lord Jesus Christ, the Old Testament was the Word of God; it was Scripture; it was something absolutely unique and apart; it had authority which nothing else has ever possessed nor can possess."[27] By these words, Lloyd-Jones affirmed the staunch position of Christ regarding the divine authority of the entire Old Testament. The Doctor realized that he must make the same commitment as did Christ to the canonical books of the Old Testament. If not, he knew he would be in opposition to the Lord.

Similarly, Lloyd-Jones recognized the same authority in the New Testament writings. This he based upon his recognition of the authority of the apostles. He stated, "The authority of the apostles undergirds and underlies the authority of the Gospels and the Epistles, the Book of Acts, indeed the whole of the New Testament. And we either accept that or we do not. It is the only authority: it is the final authority."[28] Here the New Testament is affirmed to be equally as authoritative as the Old Testament. He maintained that the Scripture is the highest word on every matter. It presides over every human

---

27. D. Martyn Lloyd-Jones, *Studies in the Sermon on the Mount* (Grand Rapids, Mich.: Eerdmans, 1959), 187.

28. Lloyd-Jones, *Authority*, 55.

opinion and trumps every cultural trend. Simply put, the Bible is the undisputed authority in all matters.

THE REFORMERS AND BIBLICAL AUTHORITY

This firm stance upon the authority of Scripture was nothing new. Lloyd-Jones knew this was an old fight for the truth, a conflict fought long ago in past centuries that must be continued today. This is an ongoing battle for the Bible that every new generation must enter. Every new hour of the church must drive down a stake for the truth of Scripture. This was the heated conflict in which the Reformers found themselves in the sixteenth century. The Protestant movement was essentially a crisis of authority in which Martin Luther, John Calvin, and others contended for *sola Scriptura*, meaning 'Scripture alone.' The issue was the sole authority in the church.

Of this hotly debated clash, Lloyd-Jones noted: "The Protestant Reformers believed not only that the Bible contained the revelation of God's truth to men, but that God safeguarded the truth by controlling the men who wrote it by the Holy Spirit, and that He kept them from error and from blemishes and from anything that was wrong."[29] Thus, he recognized: "We are having to fight once more the whole battle of the Protestant Reformation."[30] This battle for the Bible was faithfully upheld in the Westminster pulpit.

---

29. Lloyd-Jones, *The Christian Soldier*, 211.
30. Ibid., 212.

Lloyd-Jones understood this fight as a struggle between the truth and mere tradition. In this dispute, he refused to yield the high ground of biblical authority. The Doctor stated:

> It is either this Book, or else it is ultimately the author-
> ity of the Church of Rome and her "tradition"! That
> was the great issue at the Protestant Reformation. It
> was because of what they found in the Bible that those
> men stood up against, and queried and questioned
> and finally condemned the Church of Rome. It was
> that alone that enabled Luther to stand, just one man,
> defying all those twelve centuries of tradition. "I can
> do no other," he says, because of what he had found
> in the Bible.[31]

As Luther and the Reformers once stood for the exclusive authority of Scripture, Lloyd-Jones made the same firm commitment to the written Word of God. In so doing, he joined his voice with the many stalwarts of the faith who had gone before him.

MANDATING EXPOSITORY PREACHING

With penetrating vision, Lloyd-Jones saw the inseparable connection between the divine inspiration and authority

---

31. Ibid., 212.

of Scripture on the one hand and the power of expository preaching on the other hand. These two cannot be separated. It is the purity and authority of Scripture that *mandates* biblical preaching. Because the Bible is what it claims to be—the God-breathed Word that speaks with the authority of God Himself—it *must* be preached. Any man who claims to believe the Bible would be foolish to preach anything except the Word.

This is precisely how Lloyd-Jones understood the issue. He believed that the preacher is there to proclaim what God has said in His Word, nothing more:

> Any true definition of preaching must say that that man is there to deliver the message of God, a message from God to those people. If you prefer the language of Paul, he is "an ambassador for Christ." That is what he is. He has been sent, he is a commissioned person, and he is standing there as the mouthpiece of God and of Christ to address these people.[32]

There is only one way for any preacher to be a mouthpiece for God. That is to preach the written Word entrusted to him. This will be, in large measure, his inescapable accountability to God and stricter judgment on the last day.

---

32. Lloyd-Jones, *Preaching and Preachers*, 53.

IMMERSED IN SCRIPTURE

Given this mandate to preach the Word, it was necessary for Lloyd-Jones to be a man who mastered the Scripture. Consequently, his entire life was thoroughly "immersed in Scripture."[33] In his personal Bible reading, he used the Robert Murray M'Cheyne system of daily Scripture reading. He pored over four chapters of Scripture each day, two in the morning and two at night. Those who knew him best said he was like what Charles Spurgeon called John Bunyan—a walking Bible. They said that Lloyd-Jones "knew the Bible inside and out!"[34]

Lloyd-Jones believed that in preparing for a sermon, nothing is more important than being absorbed in Scripture. He challenged all preachers:

> Read your Bibles systematically. . . . I cannot emphasise too strongly the vital importance of reading the whole Bible. . . . Do not read the Bible to find texts for sermon, read it because it is the food that God has provided for your soul, because it is the Word of God, because it is the means whereby you can get to know God. Read it because it is the bread of life, the manna provided for your soul's nourishment and well-being.[35]

---

33. Christopher Catherwood, *Martyn Lloyd-Jones: A Family Portrait* (Grand Rapids, Mich.: Baker, 1994), 70.

34. Ibid.

35. Lloyd-Jones, *Preaching and Preachers*, 171–73.

Regular exposure to Scripture gave the Doctor a comprehensive grasp of the message of the entire written Word. He dug into each text to discover the doctrine taught in it. Lloyd-Jones said: "Biblical study is of very little value if it ends in and of itself and is mainly a matter of the meaning of the words. The purpose of studying the Scripture is to arrive at its doctrine."[36] This careful search in the biblical text was the basis for Lloyd-Jones being the theological expositor he was.

To best preach, Lloyd-Jones committed himself to serious study in his sermon preparation. With his commanding intellect, this master expositor devoted himself to diligently digging into the rich quarry of Scripture. In large measure, the depth of his sermon preparation determined the breadth of his ministry. The deeper he dug into the rich veins of Scripture, the higher he rose in the pulpit and, in turn, the broader was his influence upon the church and the world. Like a worker who needs not to be ashamed, Lloyd-Jones labored to mine the underground caverns of the Scripture in order to discover the vast riches of its essential meaning and key doctrines.

Lloyd-Jones honed this pattern of persistent study while a promising medical student. In that rigorous academic environment, he learned the discipline required in demanding Bible study. After this initial phase of medical study, he joined the staff of the foremost teaching hospital in the world, St. Bartholomew's Hospital in London, where he came under the

---

36. Murray, *The Fight of Faith*, 261.

tutelage of Sir Thomas Horder. There, his intellectual capacities were further sharpened by the Socratic approach of his mentor.[37] As "the most acute thinker" Horder "ever knew,"[38] Lloyd-Jones applied these same powers of study to the thorough investigation of Scripture.

Like a hard-working miner, Lloyd-Jones explored each passage until he extracted its theological gold and doctrinal gems. After he brought these treasures to the surface, he put them to use in his own daily Christian living. Out of his personal reading, he fortified his own soul. Moreover, this constant Bible study deepened his weekly sermon preparation. He was consistently being armed with biblical truth, which, in turn, he preached from the pulpit.

PRINCIPALLY, A PROCLAIMER

In an hour of growing skepticism, Lloyd-Jones believed he was primarily called to proclaim the Bible, not to defend it. He was an expositor, not an apologist. Regardless of whether anyone believed his message, his role as a preacher was to declare the truth of the Bible. From there, he would leave the results with God:

> I believe the paramount and most urgent duty at the moment is not to defend the Bible, not to argue about

---

37. Catherwood, *A Family Portrait*, 30.
38. Christopher Catherwood, *Five Evangelical Leaders* (Wheaton, Ill.: Harold Shaw, 1985), 56.

the Bible—I believe we are called upon at the present moment to declare the Bible: to announce the eternal truths contained in the Bible.[39]

Here is the genius of the preaching of Martyn Lloyd-Jones. Plain and simple, he was a Bible preacher. His supreme confidence lay in the purity and power of the Scripture, and it drove him to relentlessly preach it. He was mighty in the pulpit because he was mighty in the Word. Whatever else can be said about the preaching of this great man, this much is true: He was a powerhouse in proclaiming the Scripture. Unquestionably, God honored this man who honored His Word.

---

39. Lloyd-Jones, "The Return to the Bible," 10.

CHAPTER FOUR

Distinctly Expository

Martyn Lloyd-Jones was one of the titanic figures of twentieth-century Christianity. What now sets him apart is the fact that his writings, sermons, and other messages are even more influential now, more than two decades after his death, than when he engaged such a massive ministry at Westminster Chapel and beyond. Why? I think the answer is simple—his profound commitment to biblical exposition and the great skill with which he preached and taught the Word of God. In an age when so many preachers seem so unsure of what preaching is, in Martyn Lloyd-Jones we find a minister that leaves no doubt.[1]

—R. ALBERT MOHLER JR.

On October 6, 1977, Martyn Lloyd-Jones gave the inaugural address at the opening of the London Theological Seminary. The school was established under the Doctor's

---

1. Endorsement for Lloyd-Jones, *The Cross*.

leadership out of his great concern for the development of biblical expositors. As the founding chairman of its governing board until his death, Lloyd-Jones exerted the defining influence in crafting its vision and charting its course.

In his opening message, Lloyd-Jones laid bare his heart and addressed what he believed to be the need of the hour. He announced, "The primary need is for preachers. God has done His greatest work in the world in the church through preachers and never was there a greater need of preachers than today."[2] To this need he had given his entire life.

Lloyd-Jones stressed that the need was not for teachers, but for preachers. A teacher, he noted, "imparts information" and "passes on knowledge." He claimed, "There is less need of teachers today than there has been for a long time. This is so because the general level of culture and of knowledge is higher than it has ever been. Members of churches today, and others have had a good education."[3] He proceeded to cite his evidence for making such a statement. The many translations of Scripture, the proliferation of commentaries, and the increased literature on Christianity make the teacher less needed today to give people information. They can find this for themselves in books. Therefore, he concluded, "The greatest need is not for teaching or lecturing; it is for preaching."[4]

---

2. Martyn Lloyd-Jones, *Inaugural Address at the Opening of the London Theological Seminary* (London: London Theological Seminary, 1977), pp. 5–6.

3. Ibid., 6.

4. Ibid.

In this inaugural message, the Doctor asked, "What is preaching?" He answered, "Preaching is proclamation; it is the powerful presentation of the great message of the Bible."[5] He argued that the need of the church is for men who are able to proclaim the great message of the Bible with great power. The need is not for more information, but inspiration. "The main function of the preacher," Lloyd-Jones asserted, "is inspirational. It is not merely to dole out information, or lecture on the books of the Bible, or lecture on doctrine. He can tell people where they can read this. . . . His supreme task is to inspire the people."[6] Thus, he said, "The business of the preacher is to bring the Bible alive to them, to show them what is in it to thrill them as they hear it from him."[7] This, he believed, is the essential role of the preacher. It is making the Bible come alive in the hearts of the listeners.

The preacher, Lloyd-Jones claimed, must be a persuader who is able to move people toward Christ. Simply put, Lloyd-Jones believed the supreme need in the church is not for more teachers, as important as they are. The crying need is for preachers. This remains the case today.

Understanding the fiery preaching of Lloyd-Jones requires an apprehension of the exceedingly high view he possessed of preaching. He believed that the chief business of the church is what Paul charged Timothy with his

---

5. Ibid.
6. Ibid.
7. Ibid.

dying words, to "preach the word" (2 Tim. 4:2). Preaching must come first in the life of the church before anything else can find its rightful place. With compelling clarity, he stated, "The primary task of the Church and of the Christian minister is the preaching of the Word of God."[8] Nothing, he maintained, must ever supplant the primacy of biblical preaching in the pulpit. The Doctor believed everything in the life of the church is defined and directed by the proclamation of the Scripture.

Through the many challenges Lloyd-Jones faced, the public exposition of Scripture consistently occupied the central place in his ministry in Wales and London. In his estimation, the pulpit held the chief place in his ministry, and it was here that God used him for His glory. Through his preaching, he left an indelible imprint upon those who came to hear his expositions.

Lloyd-Jones believed that preaching worthy of the name—*biblical* preaching, *expository* preaching, *true* preaching—is the loftiest task to which anyone could commit himself. This one-time physician came to see that preaching the Word most effectively brings about the healing of the soul.

When he asked, "What is a preacher?" Lloyd-Jones replied with the following succinct description:

The first thing, obviously, is that he is a speaker. He is not primarily a writer of books, he is not an essayist

---

8. Lloyd-Jones, *Preaching and Preachers*, 19.

or a literary man; the preacher is primarily a speaker. So if the candidate has not got the gift of speech, whatever else he may have, he is not going to make a preacher. He may be a great theologian, he can be an excellent man at giving private advice and counseling, and many other things, but by basic definition, if a man has not got the gift of speech he cannot be a preacher.[9]

For Lloyd-Jones, the preacher possessed the gift of speech first and foremost, and with this gift he proclaimed the truths of Scripture. No matter how intelligent a man is or how well he knows theology, a preacher is a man with the supernatural endowment to speak divine truth in a way that is clear and compelling to the listener.

In substantiating the primacy of preaching, Lloyd-Jones pointed to the earthly ministry of Jesus Christ: "In the life and ministry of our Lord Himself, you have this clear indication of the primacy of preaching and of teaching."[10] Lloyd-Jones saw preaching as the chief activity to which the Lord devoted Himself in His public work. Christ also assigned this same priority of preaching to His Apostles. These men, Lloyd-Jones noted, were "filled with the Holy Spirit on the Day of Pentecost" and as a result, they immediately "began to preach."[11]

---

9. Ibid., 111.
10. Ibid., 21.
11. Ibid., 22.

Other pressing needs arose in the early church, yet church leaders remained focused on their primary calling. Lloyd-Jones paraphrased Peter's assertion in Acts 6:4: "We are here to preach this Word, this is the first thing, 'We will give ourselves continually to prayer and the ministry of the Word.' "[12] By this statement, Lloyd-Jones stressed that preaching the Word with prayer is the primary task of the church. He strongly asserted that these "priorities are laid down once and forever . . . and we must not allow anything to deflect us from this."[13] He believed that the priority of preaching the Word needed to be reestablished in his day.

In describing the exposition of Lloyd-Jones, Eryl Davies summarizes these messages in the following manner:

> He described all these sermons and studies as being "expository," which he believed all preaching should be. By this he meant that the preacher needed to indicate initially the relevance of the verses and then explain what they mean in their context. However, expository preaching demands even more than this, for the preacher should then open up and apply the doctrine. That was what he himself endeavoured to do in expository preaching.[14]

---

12. Ibid., 23.
13. Ibid.
14. Eryl Davies, *Dr. D. Martyn Lloyd-Jones* (Darlington, England: Evangelical, 2011), 88.

Lloyd-Jones further explained:

> Every preacher should be, as it were, at least three types or kinds of preacher. There is the preaching which is primarily evangelistic. This should take place at least once each week. There is the preaching which is instructional teaching but mainly experimental. That I generally did on a Sunday morning. There is a more purely instructional type of preaching which I personally did on a weeknight.[15]

DIVERSITY IN EXPOSITORY PREACHING

Lloyd-Jones employed different approaches in his expository preaching, depending upon when he was preaching—Sunday morning, Sunday evening, or Friday evening. This diversity in his Westminster pulpit is seen in the following ways:

Experiential Preaching

Lloyd-Jones' preaching on Sunday mornings was distinctly what he called *experiential*. In this mode, he addressed primarily believers in order to help them in living their daily Christian life. By *experiential*, he meant preaching that was geared toward assisting Christians in putting into practice their daily pursuit of Christ. Here his focus was upon teaching the Scripture in order to apply its truths to their everyday lives.

---

15. Lloyd-Jones, *Preaching and Preachers*, 63.

Lloyd-Jones' most famous series of Sunday-morning expositions was sixty consecutive sermons on the Sermon on the Mount. The series began in October 1950 and extended into 1952. Other Sunday-morning series included thirteen sermons on John 17 (1952), eleven sermons on Psalm 73 (1953), and twenty-one sermons on spiritual depression (1954).

His longest Sunday-morning preaching series was verse-by-verse through the book of Ephesians, which comprised 260 sermons (October 1954 to July 1962). In the midst of Ephesians, Lloyd-Jones paused to preach twenty-six sermons on the subject of revival (1959). The series on Ephesians was followed by a shorter series of fourteen sermons on Colossians (1962). His final Sunday-morning preaching series was in the gospel of John, in which he preached the first four chapters (1962 to 1968) until the time of his retirement.

Given the diversity of his congregation, it was always a challenge for Lloyd-Jones to reach each listener with one message. Lloyd-Jones knew he had to address each person individually with the one sermon, and he also knew that only the exposition of Scripture can address each person at their point of need. Lloyd-Jones believed that preaching should not be addressed to those who are sermon critics, but to everyday people with real needs:

Keep on reminding yourself right through from beginning to end that what you are doing is meant for people, for all sorts and kinds of people. You are not preparing a sermon for a congregation of professors or pundits; you are preparing a sermon for a mixed congregation of people, and it is your business and mine to be of some help to everybody that is in that congregation. We have failed unless we have done that. So avoid an over-academic theoretical approach. Be practical. Remember the people: you are preaching to them.[16]

Hearing Lloyd-Jones made you feel as if you were alone in a room with him and he was speaking to you face-to-face. Preaching was personal to him. He saw experiential preaching as opening up a text of Scripture and laying it bare before one's hearers. The life of each receptive hearer was then transformed by the sanctifying power of the Word.

Evangelistic Preaching

On Sunday evenings, Lloyd-Jones shaped his preaching to be *evangelistic*. This facet of his pulpit ministry was directed toward the unconverted. He determined that once each week he would bring an evangelistic message. For these sermons, he used both the Old and New Testament to encourage lost souls to come to faith in Christ. His evangelistic method was similar to his past practice as a physician, wherein he diagnosed his patients' symptoms, sought to determine the cause, and then prescribed the cure. In the pulpit, he did much the same. He began by diagnosing the sinful condition of his listeners. He

---

16. Ibid., 223.

then showed the cause—a sin nature with a depraved heart. Finally, he issued the only cure, namely, the gospel.

Concerning the need for evangelistic preaching, Lloyd-Jones believed there were always those people in his congregation who were religious but unconverted. He stated: "The main danger confronting the pulpit in this matter is to assume that all who claim to be Christians, and who think they are Christians, and who are members of the Church, are therefore of necessity Christians. This, to me, is the most fatal blunder of all."[17] As a preacher, he was compelled always to do the work of an evangelist. Scripture teaches that there will always be tares among the wheat (Matt. 13:24–30). This was his own experience as an unsaved church member. In his case, other ministers had wrongly assumed that he was converted when he was not. He resolved not to repeat this error in his pulpit ministry.

The evangelistic thrust of Lloyd-Jones' preaching was clearly witnessed by those who heard him. J.I. Packer states, "It was in his evangelism that . . . the personal electricity of his pulpit communication was unique. All his energy went into his preaching: not only animal energy, of which he had a good deal, but also the God-given liveliness . . . called unction . . . the anointing of God's Holy Spirit upon the preacher."[18] Bethan Lloyd-Jones agreed, saying, "No one will ever understand my husband until they realize that he is first of all a man

---

17. Ibid., 146.
18. Charles Turner, ed., *Chosen Vessels: Portraits of Ten Outstanding Christian Men* (Ann Arbor, Mich.: Vine, 1985), 118.

of prayer and then, an evangelist."[19] Nevertheless, he never capitulated to the techniques of modern-day evangelism by giving an altar call.

For these Sunday-evening messages, Lloyd-Jones preached consecutively through chapters in the Bible or on key topics. He delivered six sermons from Isaiah 35 (1946). This was followed by nine evangelistic sermons on Isaiah 40 (1954), seven on Psalm 107 (1955), and three on the subject of authority (1957). He also preached nine sermons on the cross from Galatians 6:14 (1963), four sermons on Psalm 1 (1963), nine sermons on Isaiah 1 (1963), and seven sermons on Isaiah 5 (1964). This led to twenty-four sermons on joy in 1964–65. His final Sunday-evening series was 110 sermons on Acts 1–8 (1965–68).

Instructional Preaching

On Friday nights, Lloyd-Jones practiced a more *instructional* mode of preaching. He started a Friday-night Bible study early in his Westminster ministry that focused primarily upon teaching Christians sound doctrines. It was preaching that demanded deeper thought in the careful scrutiny of Scripture. His first Friday-night series was on great doctrines of the Bible (eighty-one sermons, 1952–55). Far from being dry lectures, these messages were delivered with all the elements of dynamic preaching. This series was followed by his magisterial exposition of the book of Romans (372 sermons, 1957–68),

---

19. D. Martyn Lloyd-Jones, *Old Testament Evangelistic Sermons* (Edinburgh, Scotland: Banner of Truth, 1995), vii.

ending at Romans 14:17, when he retired from the Westminster pulpit.

PREACHING AND TEACHING

Whether the focus of his preaching was experiential, evangelistic, or instructional, Lloyd Jones gave himself with great diligence to each of these in sermon series. In contrasting these approaches, Curt Daniel describes Lloyd-Jones' preaching this way:

> Lloyd-Jones differentiated preaching and teaching. Campbell Morgan was a teacher, not a preacher, he would say, whereas Lloyd-Jones was a preacher and not so much a teacher. The difference is not just of approach or content, but of purpose. Teaching educates; preaching proclaims and gives transforming grace. It includes doctrine gleaned by exposition, but also application. But the middle stage is often absent from most preaching, he argued. That is the experimental, or existential, stage, when the Spirit supernaturally energizes the message, to the extent that it is biblical, and does what only He can do. Consciences are wounded, the heart is opened, grace is poured in, the soul is drawn to Christ in faith, God is glorified.[20]

---

20. Curt Daniel, *The History and Theology of Calvinism* (Springfield, Ill.: Reformed Bible Church), 162.

Hughes Oliphant Old makes this same contrast. He distinguishes in Lloyd-Jones' pulpit ministry between that which was directed more to believers and that which had unbelievers as its aim:

> His preaching at the morning service on the Lord's Day was very consciously expository, but on Sunday evening he devoted himself to evangelistic preaching. In his more mature years, the years that followed the Second World War, he was thought of as one of the leading evangelists of his day, although he was even more famous as an expository preacher. In fact, he is a beautiful example of how these two genres of preaching are at their best when combined.[21]

With this threefold approach, many would say Lloyd-Jones became, arguably, the most influential expository preacher of the twentieth century. Lloyd-Jones viewed preaching as difficult work, and therefore, if he was to say anything meaningful and transformative, he knew it required much labor. He said:

> The preparation of sermons involves sweat and labour. It can be extremely difficult at times to get all this matter that you have found in the Scriptures into this particular form. It is like a potter fashioning something out of the clay, or like a blacksmith

---

21. Old, *The Reading and Preaching of the Scriptures*, 938.

making shoes for a horse; you have to keep on putting the material into the fire and on to the anvil and hit it again and again with the hammer. Each time it is a bit better, but not quite right; so you put it back again and again until you are satisfied with it or can do no better. This is the most grueling part of the preparation of a sermon; but at the same time it is a most fascinating and a most glorious occupation.[22]

Lloyd-Jones' relentless commitment to the proclamation of the Word raised the standard for countless men who would follow after him. His style of preaching was straightforward, without any entertainment or fluff. He was structured, logical, coherent, biblical, doctrinal, fiery, urgent, declarative, and polemical. Peter Lewis describes Lloyd-Jones' preaching in the following way:

It started quietly enough: a straightforward introduction to the passage and theme before the preacher and his congregation if he were speaking to Christians, or an easy, familiar sharing of the present situation around them with its perplexities and disappointments if it were a message to non-Christians. Within a few minutes, however, quite swiftly though without dramatic suddenness there would come a deepening

---

22. Lloyd-Jones, *Preaching and Preachers*, 80.

intensity into the voice, the words quickening their pace, the body becoming the rigid, almost quivering, instrument of the speaker's fierce passion, and before one knew it one was swept into the sustained motion and progress of the whole sermon. It was, to modify a favourite story of his, the advocate taking the witness box, adding personal testimony to irrefutable argument: a man who had seen "infinities and immensities" in this Gospel concerning Jesus Christ, the Son of God, and who knew it had power to lift men and women to God for ever.[23]

ALWAYS EXPOUNDING A BIBLICAL TEXT

Lloyd-Jones understood that at the heart of his ministry was a call to preach the Bible. That is to say, he believed he was mandated by God to be an expositor. He saw it as his duty to open up the Scripture and to be a mouthpiece for the text. He said, "In preaching the message should always arise out of the Scriptures directly."[24] He further advised, "You must always be expositor. Always expository."[25] Any analysis of his preaching must begin with his unwavering commitment to the Bible itself.

The Doctor was persuaded that true preaching must always be *biblical* preaching. Lloyd-Jones said, "A sermon

23. Lewis, "The Doctor as a Preacher," 76–77.
24. Lloyd-Jones, *Preaching and Preachers*, 187.
25. Ibid., 196.

should always be expository. In a sermon the theme or the doctrine is something that arise out of the text and its context . . . a sermon should not start with the subject as such; it should start with the Scripture."[26] On this subject, he went on:

> Preparing your sermon you must begin with the exposition of your passage or single verse . . . you must be expository; and in any case my whole argument is that it should be clear to people that what we are saying is something that comes out of the Bible. We are presenting the Bible and its message . . . what we are saying comes out of the Bible, and always comes out of it. That is the origin of our message.[27]

This allegiance to expository preaching was completely foreign to most pulpits at that time in England. Iain Murray comments, "In the 1950s Lloyd-Jones was virtually alone in England in engaging in what he meant by 'expository preaching.'"[28] The Doctor did not believe that expository preaching meant giving a mere running commentary of Scripture, a string of word studies, or the grammatical structure of a text. Instead, it must present the correct principles and doctrines that the text contains.

True preaching is biblical preaching. It extracts and applies

---

26. Ibid., 71–72.
27. Ibid., 75.
28. Murray, *The Life of Martyn Lloyd-Jones*, 307.

the precepts of a text of Scripture. Murray comments, "Such preaching presents a text, then, with that text in sight throughout, there is deduction, argument, and appeal, the whole making up a message which bears the authority of Scripture itself."[29] In short, the preacher must faithfully expound the God-intended meaning of a biblical text.

A UNION OF TRUTH AND FIRE

In the Doctor, there was what Murray called "a union of truth and fire."[30] Lloyd-Jones uniquely combined the dual elements of light and heat in his preaching. Wherever there is fire, there is light and heat. The two elements are inseparable. In the fiery preaching of the Doctor, both the light of truth and the heat of passion were present.

In this regard, Murray favorably compared Lloyd-Jones with a fiery preacher of the Scottish Reformation, John Knox. He wrote, "With John Knox and his successors, he knew that the 'tongue and lively voice' are *the* chief means to which God has promised His power in the recovery of lost mankind."[31] The same can be said of Lloyd-Jones. His preaching was primary in his ministry. He believed it was through preaching that God had established His kingdom and by preaching that it best advances and functions.

---

29. Ibid.
30. Ibid, 777.
31. Ibid.

The chief end in life is the pursuit of the glory of God. This is what consumed Lloyd-Jones throughout his life. Murray points out, "His prayer for revival was accordingly associated with the profound conviction that every great movement of the Spirit will be found to be bound up with the giving of men who *preach* 'with the Holy Ghost sent down from heaven.'"[32] Preaching was constantly at the forefront of Lloyd-Jones' ministry, with the aim that God would be glorified. May the centrality of the pulpit be so recovered today in churches around the world in order that the matchless glory of God might be brilliantly showcased.

---

32. Ibid.

CHAPTER FIVE

Carefully Studied

With the death of Dr. Martyn Lloyd-Jones, the most pow-
erful and persuasive evangelical voice in Britain for some
30 years is now silent. He will be remembered chiefly as
a biblical expositor. In his heyday in the '50's and '60's at
Westminster Chapel, Buckingham Gate, he would hold
a congregation of 2,000 people spellbound for an hour
to an hour-and-a-quarter. He combined the analytical
prowess of a scientifically trained mind with the passion
of a Welshman.[1]

—JOHN STOTT

As a master craftsman knows his trade, Martyn Lloyd-Jones demonstrated the skill required to preach expositionally by realizing the difference between a lecture and a sermon. A lecture is an educational talk given in a classroom setting with the intent of transferring information from the instructor to

---

1. Catherwood, *Chosen by God*, 206.

his students. Lloyd-Jones understood that a lecture operates on a purely intellectual level with no intended emotional impact. Neither is there issued a challenge to the will. A lecture functions as a cognitive delivery of detailed facts.

On the other hand, Lloyd-Jones believed that preaching is something else entirely. "Preaching," he contended, "is not lecturing on theology."[2] A sermon is far more than a one-dimensional lecture. Though lectures can be good, they belong in a classroom, not a sanctuary. Lloyd-Jones insisted, "The business of the preacher is not to present the gospel academically."[3] Rather, a sermon is to "present the word of God to the whole man."[4] That is, the sermon must address the entire person—the mind, affections, and will. Where the lecture only instructs the mind of the listener, the sermon goes further and stirs the emotions and challenges the volition of the listener.

Pointing to the epistles of Paul, Lloyd-Jones noted they can be divided into two main sections. The Apostle begins with a doctrinal section. He then comes to a "therefore" in which he starts to apply the theology taught. "He reasons with them as to how they should live,"[5] the Doctor explains. He says, "The first half . . . is doctrinal, and the second part is practical or applicational."[6] From this, Lloyd-Jones stressed the need for the expositor to incorporate both the doctrinal

---

2. Martyn Lloyd-Jones, *Preaching and Preachers*, 65.
3. Ibid., 68.
4. Ibid.
5. Ibid., 69.
6. Ibid.

and the practical in his preaching. There must be both the teaching and application of sound doctrine. This twofold emphasis distinguishes a sermon from a lecture. The lecture has only teaching, where a sermon has teaching and application with exhortation.

In contrasting a lecture with a sermon, Lloyd-Jones said:

> I asserted that preaching a sermon is not to be confused with giving a lecture. . . . A lecture starts with a subject, and what it is concerned to do is to give knowledge and information concerning this particular subject. Its appeal is primarily and almost exclusively to the mind; its object is to give instruction and state facts."[7]

A lecture, Lloyd-Jones notes, "lacks the element of attack, the concern to do something to the listener, which is vital in preaching."[8] A sermon seeks to create an impression upon the listener, he explains, so that he is moved to feel the truth and pursue a desired course of action.

Lloyd-Jones underscored the importance of pathos in the sermon, or the arousing of the emotions. This element, he confessed, is often lacking with Reformed preachers who are highly cognitive thinkers. He stated: "We tend to lose our balance and to become over-intellectual, indeed almost to despise

---

7. Ibid.
8. Ibid., 71.

the element of feeling and emotion."[9] Being learned men, he argued, Reformed people "tend to despise feeling." They look down upon those who get emotional as those who "have no understanding." But if one can contemplate these glorious truths and remain unmoved, he concluded, "there is something defective"[10] in a person.

Lloyd-Jones believed a sermon should direct the will of the listener onto the path of personal holiness. In a sermon, the preacher should provide action steps to follow and urge the listener to pursue the prescribed will of God. A sermon is never an end in itself, but a means to a greater end. The congregation must take decisive steps of obedience to live out the Word of God. Lloyd-Jones understood that a sermon seeks to do something to the listener. He said, "He is not there merely to talk to them, he is not there to entertain them. He is there—and I want to emphasize this—to do something to those people; he is there to produce results of various kinds, he is there to influence people."[11] Therefore, the sermon, he insisted, must seek the element of producing life change in the listener.

Lloyd-Jones explained, "He is there to deal with the whole person; and his preaching is meant to affect the whole person at the very center of life."[12] This is the kind of preaching the expositor must practice.

---

9. Ibid., 93.
10. Ibid., 93–94.
11. Ibid., 53.
12. Ibid.

This being so, let us give attention to the basic steps that Lloyd-Jones undertook in order to craft an expository sermon.

ISOLATING A BIBLICAL TEXT

Lloyd-Jones believed a sermon should always be an exposition of a specific passage of Scripture. He stated, "As you start preparing your sermon you must begin with the exposition of your passage or single verse. This is essential, this is vital; as I have said, all preaching must be expository."[13] Consequently, the preacher is not to start with an idea and then elaborate upon it: "You do not start with a thought, even though it be a right thought, a good though; you do not start with that, and then work out an address on that."[14] To the contrary, the preacher must "start with the Scripture"[15] so that his message "arises out of the text."[16]

Driving home this point, the Doctor reiterated that the sermon must always be expository. What the preacher is saying, he insisted, must emerge from a biblical text:

You must be expository; and in any case my whole argument is that it should be clear to people that what we are saying is something that comes out of the Bible.

13. Ibid., 75.
14. Ibid.
15. Ibid., 72.
16. Ibid., 71.

We are presenting the Bible and its message. That is why I am one of those who like to have a pulpit Bible. It should always be there and it should always be open, to emphasise the fact that the preacher is preaching out of it.[17]

This is the beginning point of all sermon preparation. The expositor starts with a text of Scripture.

CRAFTING A SERMON OUTLINE

The next step in the process of sermon preparation is developing a sermon outline. Lloyd-Jones viewed the outline as the structure in which he could order his observations from the text. The Scripture itself clearly presents a logical form that enabled him to present its essential message. Lloyd-Jones used the sermons in the book of Acts as examples of the need for structure in a sermon. The messages there adhere to a distinct form. The Apostolic sermons are linear and follow a logical flow of thought. He commented:

You cannot read Acts 7 without being impressed by the form, the architecture, the construction, of that famous address. And surely in Paul's address in Antioch in Pisidia, as recorded in Acts 13, you find exactly the same thing. He was speaking to a plan, or

17. Ibid., 75.

if you prefer it, he had a kind of skeleton, or outline; there was certainly form to that address.[18]

Using the analogy of a human body, Lloyd-Jones saw the sermon outline like a skeleton that gives form and structure to the message. Expositors must allow their outline to come from the text. The outline keeps the preacher from presenting something the text does not say. Lloyd-Jones asserted:

These skeletons are to be clothed; they need to have flesh upon them. . . . A scaffolding is essential in putting up a building, but when you look at the completed building you do not see the scaffolding; you see the building. There is a structure there; but the structure is covered, it is only there as something to help you to put up the desired building. The same thing precisely is true of the human body. There is the frame, the skeleton; but it must be clothed with flesh before you have a body. This is equally true of a sermon.[19]

In this analogy, Lloyd-Jones viewed the sermon outline as a skeleton and the doctrine like the muscles upon the bones. Further, he viewed a person's flesh to be like the application. It is what is most seen as it lies on the surface of the bones and muscles. The skin represents how the truth is to be lived

---

18. Ibid., 74.
19. Ibid., 216–17.

by the listener. A well-proportioned human body is a thing of beauty and balance. So also should a sermon be.

Lloyd-Jones used another analogy to make his point. He also compared a sermon to a symphony. Each heading of the outline is pictured by the major divisions of the symphony. He explained:

> I maintain that a sermon should have form in the sense that a musical symphony has form. A symphony always has form, it has its parts and its portions. The divisions are clear, and are recognized, and can be described; and yet a symphony is a whole. . . . One should always think of a sermon as a construction, a work which is in that way comparable to a symphony. In other words a sermon is not a mere meandering through a number of verses; it is not a mere collection or series of excellent and true statement and remarks. . . . What makes a sermon a sermon is that it has this particular "form" which differentiates it from everything else.[20]

Lloyd-Jones was explicit that the sermon divisions are not to be placed in random order. To the contrary, these headings must be arranged in a logical sequence that best presents the particular doctrine that the text teaches. Therefore, the

---

20. Ibid., 72–73.

preacher must position his headings so that the first point leads seamlessly to the second point, and so on. Lloyd-Jones said, "Each one should lead to the next, and work ultimately to a definite conclusion. Everything is to be argued as to bring out the main thrust of this particular doctrine."[21] This expository outline establishes the orderly structure that should direct the presentation in a sermon.

Lloyd-Jones believed there must be a logical progression of thought throughout the entire sermon that builds to a climax. The points in the outline should be interrelated and interdependent. Each heading is simply a part of the whole and should be "aiming at an ultimate conclusion."[22] Much like multiple streams converging together to form one fast-moving river, the various parts of the sermon outline, he believed, should flow together into one larger body of thought. The important truths should stand out in the sermon and be lodged in the mind of the listener. So important is this orderly structure to an effective sermon that the Doctor commented, "If my sermon is not clear and ordered in my mind I cannot preach it to others."[23] The sermon must be clear to the one in the pulpit before it can be lucid to those in the pews.

To underscore the importance of the outline, Lloyd-Jones used Jonathan Edwards as an example. He recognized that in his later years, Edwards did not write out his full manuscript.

---

21. Ibid., 77.
22. Ibid.
23. Ibid., 211.

He nevertheless still saw the necessity of composing a sermon outline. As Edwards matured in his preaching, his manuscript grew smaller until he carried only a thin outline into the pulpit. But the great preacher of the Great Awakening never preached without at least an outline. Thus, Lloyd-Jones noted the critical importance of the sermon outline to Edwards:

> Jonathan Edwards is most interesting in this respect. Until recently I was always under the impression that Edwards always wrote out all his sermons in full. It is quite certain that in his early days he did so, and that furthermore he actually read them in the pulpit to the people. . . . As Edwards went on he did not write his sermons in full, but contented himself with writing some notes. . . . It is always wrong to lay down absolute laws in these matters. . . . I felt that writing was good discipline, good for producing ordered thought and arrangement and sequence and development of the argument and so on.[24]

The outline's importance stems from its being a means to an end. It is most critical to arrange one's thoughts to clearly present the argument of the text. The outline exists, Lloyd-Jones concluded, solely to serve this greater purpose. Lloyd-Jones was careful to point out that an outline should

---

24. Ibid., 215.

not be a collection of individual parts. Rather, it forms the structure of a message and shapes its presentation. A well-prepared outline provides the preacher with an entire unit of thought to be presented.

LOCATING THE MAIN IDEA

Lloyd-Jones realized the expositor must capture the central thrust of his text. He called the main idea of the sermon the "doctrine." Lloyd-Jones believed that if one properly understands the text, he will discover its core teaching and its place in the larger message of the Bible. He conceded this is sometimes the most difficult and time-consuming work of sermon preparation. Nevertheless, isolating its specific teaching can be the most important part in developing a good message.

In discovering the main idea, Lloyd-Jones knew the expositor must ask himself questions concerning the intentions of his text's author: "Why did he say that? Why did he say it in this particular way? What is he getting at? What was his object and purpose?"[25] These diagnostic questions probe the text and reveal the central thrust of the passage.

Likewise, the larger body of doctrine taught in the entire Bible should govern the interpretation of each selected text. He stated, "[The preacher's] interpretation of any particular text should be checked and controlled by this system, this

---

25. Ibid., 202.

body of doctrine and of truth which is found in the Bible."[26] The main idea of the sermon is enhanced by this comprehensive knowledge of the whole Scripture.

Lloyd-Jones was amazed at how many modern preachers miss the main idea of the text. During a six-month season of illness, he recounted listening to many sermons and noted with sadness that very few preachers arrived at the central idea of the text. In most cases, the preacher altogether missed the core teaching of the text. One such sermon he heard was on Romans 1:1–4 on Easter Sunday. The preacher emphasized Jesus as the Son of God, but he went away from the sermon "without a sense of astonishment at the amazing event of the Resurrection, the things which according to the Apostle finally 'declared' Him to be 'the Son of God.'"[27] The thrust of Paul's message was not the same made by this preacher who delivered the sermon. Therefore, in Lloyd-Jones' estimation, he missed the central point of what Paul was saying.

Lloyd-Jones also warned of the danger of failing to see the context in which the passage finds itself. This can also cause a preacher to miss the main idea of the text. He said "a misunderstanding of the particular verse" often occurs "because of a complete ignoring of the previous and the following verses."[28] In other words, the larger perspective of a passage is critical in gaining its proper insight. He said, "I cannot over-emphasise

26. Ibid., 66.
27. Ibid., 203.
28. Ibid., 204.

the importance of our arriving at the main thrust, the main message of our text. Let it lead you, let it teach you. Listen to it and then question it as to its meaning, and let that be the burden of your sermon."[29] The preacher must grasp the intent of the biblical author in order to capture and convey what God says in His Word.

USING LINGUISTIC TOOLS

In scrutinizing Scripture, Lloyd-Jones insisted that his analysis should include studying a text in the original languages in order to arrive at the precise interpretation. He stated that the Greek and Hebrew "are of great value for the sake of accuracy; no more, that is all."[30] He cautioned, "They cannot guarantee accuracy, but they promote it."[31] In other words, far more is involved in rightly handling a passage of Scripture than understanding the original language.

Mainly, Lloyd-Jones stressed that an entry-level knowledge of the original languages is helpful in using technical commentaries, which exegete texts in Greek and Hebrew. In the opening address of London Theological Seminary, he stated, "What is needed by preachers today is a sufficient knowledge of Greek and Hebrew to enable them to use their Commentaries, and to read the many translations available

---

29. Ibid.
30. Ibid., 116.
31. Ibid.

in an intelligent manner, and to be able to follow the argumentation of the authorities for one view rather than another."[32] Thus, the original languages should be learned primarily to aid in the use of commentaries for interpreting the Scripture.

It is wrong, however, to say a man cannot preach if he lacks a sufficient knowledge of the original languages, he said. "To say that a man cannot read his Bible, and that he cannot preach if he lacks a knowledge of Greek and Hebrew seems to me a serious misunderstanding of the biblical message, and the true character of preaching."[33] Instead, "what is needed is this basic knowledge of these languages."[34] This was certainly a difference from the prevailing opinion of the time.

Consulting the Commentaries

After digging into the text, Lloyd-Jones then urged a preacher to use "commentaries or any aids that you may choose to employ."[35] Lloyd-Jones had a significant personal library in his study. In fact, the Banner of Truth Trust had its beginnings in reprinting some of his most rare Puritan books. This library remains housed in the London Theological Seminary. As a doctor seeks the opinion of another examining physician,

---

32. Lloyd-Jones, *Inaugural Address*, 12.
33. Ibid.
34. Ibid.
35. Lloyd-Jones, *Preaching and Preachers*, 171–73.

so Lloyd-Jones consulted these commentaries as a reference point in his sermon preparation.

It is also necessary, Lloyd-Jones insisted, that the preacher never force his text to say something it does not say. To do so would be to practice *eisegesis*, or reading into the text what is not there, rather than *exegesis*, which is pulling the teachings out of the text. He warned, "You must sacrifice a good sermon rather than force a text."[36] To avoid this pitfall, the Doctor recommended consulting commentaries to make sure one's conclusions as to the thrust and core doctrine of the passage line up with those of other faithful men.

MAKING THE APPLICATION

After arriving at the doctrine of the text, Lloyd-Jones empha-sized that the preacher must show its practical relevance for daily living to the congregation. This meant keeping in mind how the text should affect those sitting in the pew. The preacher must keep before him the needs of his listeners in order to connect the message to their individual lives. This means that the expositor "has to assess the condition of those in the pew and to bear that in mind in the preparation and delivery of his message."[37] In other words, he must exegete both the text and his listeners in order to stand between these two worlds.

---

36. Ibid., 202.
37. Ibid., 143.

During his sermon preparation, the preacher must be keenly aware of who his audience is. That is, he must discern their condition and be in tune with the needs of his listeners. He emphasized that he said what he did because he was influenced by the condition of the people. The Word is to be preached to real people in the world who live in real-life situations.

The preacher must also keep in mind the fundamental rule of assessing the listening and learning capacity of his hearers. Lloyd-Jones said, "The chief fault of the young preacher is to preach to the people as we would like them to be, instead of as they are."[38] There is a tendency to forget that the great preachers one reads in sermon preparation were from another time and era. He cautioned that they had hearers who were taught and trained to listen in different ways from the modern world. We cannot preach while giving no thought to the context of our hearers. The job of the preacher is to present the text in such a way that its relevance is clearly seen and easily applied by the congregation.

Lloyd-Jones aptly stressed, "You are not lecturing, you are not reading an essay; you are setting out to do something definite and particular, to influence these people and the whole of their lives and outlook."[39] He pointed out:

> You are not an antiquary lecturing on ancient history
> or on ancient civilisations, or something like that.

---

38. Ibid., 144.
39. Ibid., 76.

The preacher is a man who is speaking to people who are alive today and confronted by the problems of life; and therefore you have to show that this is not some academic or theoretical matter which may be of interest to people who take up that particular hobby, as others take up crossword puzzles or something of that type. You are to show that this message is vitally important for them, and that they must listen with the whole of their being, because this really is going to help them to live.[40]

INCLUDING THE ILLUSTRATIONS

Lloyd-Jones believed in using illustrations, but only in a restricted manner. He stressed that illustrations should come naturally to the preacher without exerting a strenuous effort in finding them. He challenged the use of illustration books as "a kind of abomination." Some illustrations are used to falsely gain the attention of his listeners. He went so far as to compare searching for illustrations to match one's point to a prostitute's luring someone in through seduction.[41] It is far better, Lloyd-Jones said, to use illustrations from one's knowledge of Scripture and church history than to steal them from others.

---

40. Ibid., 76.
41. Ben Bailie, "Lloyd-Jones and the Demise of Preaching," in *Engaging with Martyn Lloyd-Jones,* eds. Andrew Atherstone and David Ceri Jones (Nottingham, England: InterVarsity, 2011), 166.

In addition, Lloyd-Jones stressed that the illustration should be subservient to the truth. The doctrine being taught is the master, while the illustration is the slave. Too many preachers, he believed, were using illustrations to entertain the listeners rather than to establish the point of the text. He stated:

> The illustration is meant to illustrate truth, not to show itself, not to call attention to itself; it is a means of leading and helping people to see the truth that you are enunciating and proclaiming still more clearly. The rule therefore should always be that the truth must be pre-eminent and have great prominence, and illustrations must be used sparsely and carefully to that end alone. Our business is not to entertain people. People like stories, they like illustrations. I have never understood why, but people seem to like ministers who are always talking about their own families. I always find that very boring when I am listening, and I cannot understand a preacher who likes doing that. Surely there is a good deal of conceit about it. Why should people be more interested in the preacher's children than in those of other people? They have their own children and they could multiply such stories equally well themselves. The argument for this, generally, is that it introduces "a personal touch." . . . You can well see how it can pander to that which is lowest and worst in many members of the congregation. It is sheer

carnality, a kind of lust and desire to know personal details about people. But a preacher should go into a pulpit to enunciate and proclaim the Truth itself. This is what should be prominent, and everything else is but to minister to this end. Illustrations are just servants, and you should use them sparsely and carefully.[42]

SUPPLYING THE QUOTATIONS

Lloyd-Jones urged the limited use of quotations in the sermon. He reasoned that people have come to hear the preacher standing before them, not someone else from another era. He cautioned, "Too many quotations in a sermon become very wearisome to the listener, and at times they can even be ridiculous."[43]

> A sermon is meant to be a proclamation of the truth of God as mediated through the preacher. People do not want to listen to a string of quotations of what other people have thought and said. They have come to listen to you; you are the man of God, you have been called to the ministry, you have been ordained; and they want to hear this great truth as it comes through you, through the whole of your being.[44]

---

42. Ibid., 232–34.
43. Lloyd-Jones, *Preaching and Preachers*, 222.
44. Ibid., 222.

The use of a lengthy quotation or a long list of multiple quotations should be restricted, Lloyd-Jones believed. The preacher must preach in such a manner that his own voice is heard, not that of someone else. The people need to feel his concern for their souls. They need to see his desire for their spiritual growth.

Writing the Introduction

The sermon introduction, according to Lloyd-Jones, can make or break the delivery. The beginning serves as the front door to the exposition. Therefore, it makes a first impression upon the listener and should be given careful consideration. There are certain characteristics of the opening part of a sermon that must be understood before it can be rightly written.

If the sermon is a part of a series, the Doctor felt an effective introduction should contain a summary of the previous exposition. It likewise should indicate the various divisions of this particular sermon that the listener will be hearing in this message. Lloyd-Jones said:

Take a few minutes at the beginning of the sermon in which to give a brief resume of what you have been saying previously. I emphasise the word "brief." . . . Though that tendency to be too long in giving a synopsis of the previous sermon must be firmly resisted, a summary is nevertheless essential for the people. It will help all of them, even those who attend regularly; and for strangers who may attend, it is essential.[45]

In the introduction, Lloyd-Jones stated, "The preacher should indicate the main theme and its various divisions in his general introduction."[46] Here, the preacher should whet the appetite of the hearers and create a desire for them to learn what is in the passage. At the same time, he must not say too much and give away the main details of what he will be saying. If he does, the listener will become bored during the sermon itself. The introduction should also be relatively short without unnecessarily tiring the listener. For instance, Lloyd-Jones said:

> I have known sermons that have almost exhausted me in the introduction, and it has taken me a long time to get to know them and understand them so that I can handle them correctly, instead of their handling me and running away with me. Many a time I have known sermons that have so carried me away in the introduction that when I came to what was really important, and especially to the climax, I found I was already tired out and exhausted and could not do justice to the matter.[47]

45. Ibid., 198–99.
46. Ibid., 76.
47. Ibid., 292.

Lloyd-Jones maintained that the preacher should not exhaust his hearers by diving too deeply into the explanation of the text in the introduction. The purpose of the introduction is to serve as a doorway into the instruction of the sermon. The goal is not to say everything in the introduction but to provide incentive to hear the main body of the message by showing its importance to the listener.

DRAFTING THE CONCLUSION

Regarding the conclusion, Lloyd-Jones also reinforced its strategic importance to a good sermon. He said, "You must end on a climax, and everything should lead up to it in such a way that the great truth stands out dominating everything that has been said, and the listeners go away with this in their minds."[48] The expositor must treat every conclusion as his final word to his hearers. There are some listeners who may never hear a message from God's Word again. The preacher must be fully aware of the seriousness of the opportunity to exposit the Scriptures.

The conclusion is where the preacher urges his listeners to act upon the truth they have heard. According to Lloyd-Jones, this response to the sermon does not involve walking an aisle during an invitation. Instead, the desired outcome depends upon a clear presentation of the gospel of Christ and bringing

---

48. Ibid., 77.

the truth of the sermon to bear upon the lives of the hearers. Ultimately, the success is in the hands of the Holy Spirit, who alone grants repentance and faith. Lloyd-Jones repeatedly affirmed this reliance upon the Spirit when he said:

> This is the work of the Holy Spirit of God. His work is a thorough work, it is a lasting work; and so we must not yield to this over-anxiety about results. I am not saying it is dishonest, I say it is mistaken. We must learn to trust the Spirit and to rely upon His infallible work.[49]

This is where the confidence of the preacher should always lie. His certainty must be in the sovereign activity of the Holy Spirit to apply the Word to the heart of the listener. In the end, God will honor the man who honors His Word.

SEEKING GOD'S APPROVAL

As the preacher prepares his message, it is critical that God be the one directing what he writes. Many a pastor develops his message with the desire to win the approval of his listeners. This leads him to become a man-pleaser in the sermon who attempts to tickle ears. Lloyd-Jones emphasized, "I would lay it down as being axiomatic that the pew is never to dictate

---

49. Ibid., 282.

to, or control, the pulpit." [50] The preacher must always be a God-pleaser.

Lloyd-Jones said that when he was a physician, he never allowed the patient to write the prescription. As the attending doctor, he knew what was best for the one in need of care. So it was in ministry for the Doctor. He sought the Lord on behalf of his congregation and lovingly gave them the truth that they needed for the health of their souls. Even so, every preacher in this hour, must be led by God regarding what they prepare to preach. Only God-pleasers make excellent expositors.

---

50. Ibid., 143.

CHAPTER SIX

Divinely
Focused

*I was able to hear Dr. Lloyd-Jones preach his way through
Matthew 11. I had never heard such preaching and was
electrified. I can remember at least the thrust of most of
the messages still. . . . All that I know about preaching
I can honestly say—indeed, have often said—I learned
from the Doctor by example that winter.*[1]

—J.I. PACKER

As a twenty-two-year-old student in London, the noted
theologian J.I. Packer visited Westminster Chapel on
Sunday evenings to hear Martyn Lloyd-Jones preach. This
firsthand exposure to the pulpit ministry of Lloyd-Jones came
during the school year of 1948–49 when Packer had been
a Christian for only four years. The effect of Lloyd-Jones'
preaching upon Packer's early Christian life was incalculable.

---

1. Murray, *The Fight of Faith*, 188.

Packer later reflected upon this encounter with the Doctor's preaching:

> The preacher was a small man with a big head and evidently thinning hair, wearing a shapeless-looking black gown. His great domed forehead caught the eye at once. He walked briskly to the little pulpit desk in the centre of the balcony, said "Let us pray" in a rather pinched, deep, Welsh-inflected, microphone-magnified voice, and at once began pleading with God to visit us during the service. The blend of reverence and intimacy, adoration and dependence, fluency and simplicity in his praying was remarkable: he had a great gift in prayer. Soon he was reading a Bible chapter (Matthew 11), briskly and intelligently rather than dramatically or weightily; and in due course the auditorium lights went out and he launched into a 45-minute sermon. . . . The sermon (as we say nowadays) blew me away.[2]

Packer explains the sermon delivery in this manner:

> What was special about it? It was simple, clear, straightforward man-to-man stuff. It was expository, apologetic, and evangelistic on the grand scale. It was both the planned performance of a magnetic orator and

---

2. D. Martyn Lloyd-Jones, *The Heart of the Gospel* (Wheaton, Ill.: Crossway, 1991), 7–8.

the passionate, compassionate outflow of a man with a message from God that he knew his hearers needed. He worked up to a dramatic growling shout about God's sovereign grace a few minutes before the end; then from that he worked down to businesslike persuasion, calling on needy souls to come to Christ. It was the old, old story, but it had been made wonderfully new. I went out full of awe and joy, with a more vivid sense of the greatness of God in my heart than I had known before.[3]

Looking back upon those years, Packer describes the powerful impact of Lloyd-Jones' preaching this way: "I have never heard another preacher with so much of God about him. . . . In conclusion, he points us to the God of all grace."[4] Herein lies the true greatness of the preaching of Lloyd-Jones. To those who sat under its force, his biblical expositions conveyed a sense of the living God. Far from being a mere dead orthodoxy, the Doctor's preaching was high voltage, that surged with a currency of life-changing spiritual power that manifested the awesomeness of God.

DEVOTED TO THE PERSON OF GOD

The spiritual power transmitted by Lloyd-Jones' preaching grew out of his own transcendent view of God. No man's preaching

---

3. Ibid., 8.
4. Murray, *The Fight of Faith*, 325.

can rise any higher than his view of God. The sheer genius of Lloyd-Jones' preaching was based on his strong piety and personal knowledge of God and His Word. The more he exalted God in the pulpit, the higher the people rose in their worship of God. He was constantly magnifying the glory of God and leading his listeners to behold His greatness, love, and grace.

In 1969, Lloyd-Jones delivered a series of lectures on preaching at Westminster Theological Seminary. There, he asserted:

> Preaching is first of all a proclamation of the being of God . . . preaching worthy of the name starts with God and with a declaration concerning His being and power and glory. You find that everywhere in the New Testament. That was precisely what Paul did in Athens—"Him declare I unto you." "Him"! Preaching about God, and contrasting Him with the idols, exposing the emptiness and the acuity and uselessness of idols.[5]

True biblical preaching comes directly from God, Lloyd-Jones affirmed, and the preacher is only the messenger who is empowered by the Holy Spirit and undergirded by fervent prayer. This is precisely where he chose to focus his expositions. The Doctor looked for the grandeur of God in every text and sought to magnify Him above all else. He was constantly elevating God to the highest priority in his pulpit ministry. Even

---

5. Lloyd-Jones, *Preaching and Preachers*, 62–63.

as he listened to other men preach, he was willing to overlook their mediocre delivery or disorganized presentation if the man could simply convey a true sense of the greatness of God.

> I can forgive a man a bad sermon, I can forgive the preacher almost anything if he gives me a sense of God, if he gives me something for my soul, if he gives me the sense that though he is inadequate in himself, he is handling something which is very great and glorious, if he gives me some dim glimpse of the majesty and glory of God, the love of Christ my Saviour, and the magnificence of the gospel. If he does that, I am his debtor, and I am profoundly grateful to him.[6]

Lloyd-Jones believed the focus of the sermon is to unveil God. Asking himself the question, "What is the chief end of preaching?" he succinctly answered, "I like to think it is this. It is to give men and women a sense of God and His presence."[7] This is the very essence of what Lloyd-Jones understood authentic preaching to be. He believed it is to be an exaltational exposition, that is, preaching that is always exalting God.

Simply put, Lloyd-Jones believed the primary purpose of the Word of God is to reveal the God of the Word. He firmly believed the goal of the pulpit is not to place the focus upon the culture or any particular social cause. Neither was

---

6. Ibid., 98.
7. Ibid., 97.

the spotlight to be placed upon the political scene of the day. Rather, the focus of biblical preaching is to be upon the attributes and activities of God. This theocentric focus was the unmistakable priority of his pulpit ministry.

More than anything else, those who heard Lloyd-Jones preach left the worship service with their hearts filled with fervent praise to God and humbled in the sight of His holiness. He was always pointing his listeners upward to God. He exhorted them:

> Let us not stop at any benefit we may have had, and not even with the highest experiences we may have enjoyed. Let us seek to know more and more of the glory of God. That is what leads always to a true experience. We need to know the majesty of God, the sovereignty of God, and to feel a sense of awe and of wonder. Do we know this? Is there in our churches a sense of wonder and amazement?[8]

For Lloyd-Jones, the highest goal of preaching is not found in merely transferring intellectual content or making an emotional impact. These are important, but they are the effect, not the cause. The goal of preaching is to plant within people the knowledge of God, a sense of wonder for His divine holiness, and an overwhelming realization of His ardent love for sinners.

---

8. D. Martyn Lloyd-Jones, *The Puritans: Their Origins and Successors* (Edinburgh, Scotland: Banner of Truth, 2014), 120.

In this sense, Lloyd-Jones viewed himself as the "worship leader." The one who makes God known to the flock, he maintained, is the one who leads in worship. This title should be reserved for the one who exposits the Word. Lloyd-Jones noted, "The goal of all of our seeking and all our worship and all our endeavour should not be to have a particular experience; it should not be to petition certain blessings; it should be to know God Himself—the Giver not the gift, the source and the fount of every blessing, not the blessing itself."[9] This was the essential effect which he sought to instill in his listeners. Exposition must always lead to adoration.

After hearing Lloyd-Jones preach, one listener, Leigh B. Powell, was overwhelmed by the greatness of God. He stated that one would hardly dare to breathe for fear of missing a word that magnified the Almighty. Describing this God-centered preaching, Powell stated:

His heart passionately sought after this manifestation of the glory of God. He longed to see the fire descend upon the altar of his preaching—that heavenly unction that convinces all men that God is in the midst of His people—and that to bless. At times—often toward the end of a sermon, he seemed to be hovering, waiting for something. Sometimes the wind of the Spirit would come sweep us and him aloft, and we

---

9. Lloyd-Jones, *Great Doctrines*, 50.

would mount with wings like eagles into the awesome and felt presence of God.[10]

It is obvious that Lloyd-Jones desired to be greatly used by God and empowered by the Holy Spirit, such that the effect of his preaching would be due not to his own persuasive words or planning but to the power of the Spirit. His desire was to show the people the radiant love of God that penetrates the deepest sin and rescues the hell-bound sinner. He believed preaching must begin with who God is and then proceed to man. It must not start with man and then move to God. It was in first seeing God that a man rightly sees himself. Only then can anyone understand what his true needs are. Only in the knowledge of God can an individual see how to live. Therefore, Lloyd-Jones was convinced that all preaching must, first and foremost, recognize God's preeminence.

The entire message of the Bible, Lloyd-Jones saw, begins and ends with God. The Bible is far more than an instruction manual for living a good life. The Word of God is, first and foremost, a presentation of the awesome majesty of God. He exclaimed:

This is a staggering thought but it is entirely consistent with the whole of biblical teaching. It is just here that we all tend to go astray. Although we have the

---

10. Catherwood, *Chosen by God*, 87.

open Bible before us we still tend to base our ideas of doctrine on our own thoughts instead of on the Bible. The Bible always starts with God the Father; and we must not start anywhere else, or with anyone else.[11]

If an expositor begins with any emphasis other than with God Himself, the sermon is certain to go astray. Starting with the very first verse of the Bible, the message of Scripture is the presentation of the attributes and actions of God. Lloyd-Jones maintained:

The Bible starts with God; you remember its great opening statement which really tells us everything: "In the beginning God. . . ." The knowledge of God is ultimately the sum of all other doctrines; there is no sense, there is no meaning or purpose, in any other doctrine apart from this great central, all-inclusive, doctrine of God Himself. There is no point in considering the doctrine of salvation, nor the doctrine of sin, unless we have started with the doctrine of God.[12]

For Lloyd-Jones, the mandate of Scripture is to unveil the person of God. All other doctrines are best seen and understood in the light of a proper knowledge of God. Theology

11. D. Martyn Lloyd-Jones, *God's Ultimate Purpose: An Exposition of Ephesians 1:1–23* (Grand Rapids, Mich.: Baker, 1978), 82.
12. Lloyd-Jones, *Great Doctrines*, 47.

proper—the study of God Himself—is the ultimate paradigm through which one sees every other area of theology. Unless the majesty of God is the priority of every pulpit, other doctrines will be misperceived by the hearer. Therefore, Lloyd-Jones believed God must be the beginning, middle, and end of all preaching.

DEVOTED TO THE HOLINESS OF GOD

The preaching of God must begin with expounding the absolute holiness of God. Lloyd-Jones said every other area of truth must be viewed in light of this divine attribute. No other aspect of God's character takes precedence over this fundamental truth. God is holy, absolutely perfect in His being and ways. Lloyd-Jones asserted, "The Bible teaches us everywhere that God is holy, and part of the manifestation of this holiness is His hatred of sin and His separation from sin, from the sinners and from all that is evil."[13] The Doctor stressed that God is high and lifted up, transcendent, morally blameless, flawless, and separated from sinners. This must be the beginning place for all preaching.

Lloyd-Jones believed that the primacy of divine holiness must be continually declared in the pulpit. The knowledge of God's holiness is necessary to reveal the sinfulness of man and his just condemnation by God. The holiness of God, he

---

13. Ibid., 69.

maintained, should be a cause for a healthy, reverential fear before God. He wrote:

> The purpose of the biblical revelation of God's holiness is to teach us how to approach Him. It is not mere theoretical knowledge that we are asked to try to grasp with our understandings. Its purpose is very practical. In the words of the author of the epistle of Hebrews, we are to approach God "with reverence and godly fear" (Hebrews 12:28). He is always to be approached in that way, wherever you are; when you are alone in a room, or when you are meeting as a family to pray, or when you are in a public service, God is always God and He is always to be approached "with reverence and godly fear."[14]

The knowledge of God's holiness, Lloyd-Jones maintained, provides listeners with a deep awareness of their own sin. He stated, "You will never have a knowledge of sin unless you have a true conception of the holiness of God."[15] The preaching of divine holiness makes the knowledge of sin real and arrests the soul before God.

The pulpit must likewise present the only basis by which sinful man can approach God. It is the realization of divine holiness that makes the atonement of Christ necessary.

---

14. Ibid., 71.
15. Ibid.

Lloyd-Jones exclaimed: "God's holiness shows us the absolute necessity of the atonement. . . . Without the shedding of blood there is no remission of sin, that God's holiness insists upon it, demands an atonement for sin."[16] In other words, the holiness of God mandates the cross.

Lloyd-Jones rebutted those who chose to begin their preaching with divine love. He addressed their objections when he said, "'Why,' asks someone, 'is it so vital that we must start with God and not ourselves; why do we start with God and not with our opinions? Why must I be so attuned to this revelation? Why must I start with the holiness of God rather than with His love?'"[17] This is the decisive question in any pulpit ministry. In answering this liberal challenge, Lloyd-Jones asserted: "Let me give you some answers. I suggest that if you do not start with the holiness of God you will never understand God's plan of salvation, which is that salvation is only possible to us through the death of our Lord Jesus Christ on the cross on Calvary's hill."[18] To this, Lloyd-Jones explained why the cross is absolutely necessary. There is no other way for unholy sinners to find acceptance with a holy God. He maintained:

> But the question arises, why is that cross essential, why is that the only way whereby man can be saved? If God is only love and compassion and mercy, then

16. Ibid., 72.

17. D. Martyn Lloyd-Jones, *Life in Christ: Studies in 1 John* (Wheaton, Ill.: Crossway, 2002), 101.

18. Ibid.

the cross is surely meaningless, for if God is love alone, then all He needs to do when man sins is to forgive him. But the whole message is that the cross is at the center, and without that death God, I say with reverence, cannot forgive.[19]

To fail to present the holiness of God is to strip the cross of Christ of its true meaning. He continued:

It is the holiness of God that demands the cross, so without starting with holiness there is no meaning in the cross. It is not surprising that the cross has been discounted by modern theologians; it is because they have started with the love of God without His holiness. It is because they have forgotten the life of God, His holy life, that everything in Him is holy; with God love and forgiveness are not things of weakness or compromise. He can only forgive sin as He has dealt with it in His own holy manner, and that is what He did upon the cross.[20]

If God is not holy, Lloyd-Jones argues, the cross is unnecessary and has no power whatsoever to forgive sin. Forfeiting the high ground of divine holiness is to rob the cross of its power to save. No expositor can rightly preach the love of God

19. Ibid.
20. Ibid.

without first expounding His holiness. From this foundation, Lloyd-Jones would not be moved. No preacher can proclaim the gospel with converting power without first establishing God's holiness. Lloyd-Jones concludes by stating:

> Therefore it is essential to start with the holiness of God; otherwise the plan of redemption, the scheme of salvation, becomes meaningless and we can see no point or purpose in some of the central doctrines of the Christian faith. But if I start with the holiness of God I see that the incarnation must take place; the cross is absolutely essential, and the resurrection and the coming of the Holy Spirit and every other part of the great plan as well. How important it is that we should start at the right place; how vital it is that we should be led by truth and not by our own ideas.[21]

Resisting the prevailing liberalism, Lloyd-Jones maintained that when the preacher contends for the holiness of God, all other doctrines fall into their proper place. God's transcendent purity shines brightly and puts all other truths in the right light. The principal duty of every preacher, Lloyd-Jones believed, is to proclaim the holiness of God. Only then does one see his sin and sense his condemnation before God. Only then can one grasp the necessity of the cross. Only then will

---

21. Ibid.

one see his dire need for the righteousness of Christ. Without understanding the holiness of God, Lloyd-Jones believed that the doctrines of salvation cannot be rightly grasped. This is the starting place for gospel preaching. Lloyd-Jones said:

> Our business, our work, our first call is to declare in a certain and unequivocal manner the sovereignty, the majesty, and the holiness of God; the sinfulness and the utter depravity of man, and his total inability to save and to rescue himself; and the sacrificial, expiatory, atoning death of Jesus Christ, the Son of God, on that cross on Calvary's hill, and His glorious resurrection, as the only means and only hope of human salvation.[22]

DEVOTED TO THE GLORY OF GOD

Moreover, Lloyd-Jones insisted that the preacher must proclaim the glory of God. He defines the glory of God as "the essential nature of God; it is that which makes God God."[23] The glory of God is the sum and substance of who God is. No one can add anything to God's intrinsic glory. Nor can anyone take away from it. The glory of God is never increasing, nor decreasing. It is forever the same. Concerning this truth, Lloyd-Jones noted:

22. Lloyd-Jones, "The Return to the Bible," 11.
23. Lloyd-Jones, *God's Ultimate Purpose*, 130.

> If there is one term which describes God more than any other it is this term "glory." It includes beauty, majesty, or better still, splendor. It also includes the idea of greatness and might and eternity. All these terms are included in this one term "glory." We cannot go beyond it.[24]

Lloyd-Jones believed that the responsibility of the preacher is to proclaim the glory of God, which "is displayed in everything that God does."[25] To preach God necessitates preaching His glory in creation, history, and salvation. Lloyd-Jones affirmed, "In the Lord Jesus Christ we see the glory of God at its greatest height."[26] He added: "When the Son of God came into this world, above all else He was revealing the glory of God. 'And we beheld His glory' (John 1:14)."[27] Consequently, this Westminster expositor contended, "We must emphasize that our salvation is the greatest and highest manifestation of the glory of God."[28] To preach the glory of God is to proclaim the gospel of grace.

The chief responsibility of the preacher is to preach the glory of God in the cross of Christ. To expound the glory of God is to set forth His saving splendor in the pulpit. The highest aim of preaching is to display the greatness of God

---

24. Ibid.
25. Ibid.
26. Ibid., 133.
27. Ibid., 131.
28. Ibid., 132.

in the salvation purchased by Jesus Christ and offered freely to sinners.

THE INEXHAUSTIBLE SUBJECT

Lloyd-Jones knew the preacher would never exhaust a subject so vast as the infinite glory of God. Neither will the congregation ever tire of hearing about His incomprehensible majesty. Lloyd-Jones exclaimed, "As I understand the teaching of the Bible, and as seems quite inevitable from the nature and being of God, it is a theme which will occupy God's people throughout the endless ages of eternity."[29] Throughout the ages to come, it is upon the glory of God that believers will focus their attention and adoration. No preacher will ever plumb the depths of this inexhaustible subject. Preaching God is a body of divinity so vast that He can never be fully discovered. Thus, Lloyd-Jones contended that the focus of preaching should prioritize the proclamation of who God is rather than upon what He can give.

In this matter, Lloyd-Jones also believed that a preacher should not invest his efforts in explaining the existence of God in the face of an unbelieving world. Instead, he must focus his energies upon declaring the all-glorious being of God. He stated: "The Bible does not argue about the existence of God; it declares it. The Bible does not give us any proofs of

29. Lloyd-Jones, *Great Doctrines*, 48.

the existence of God; it assumes it."[30] As Lloyd-Jones stepped into the pulpit, he gave himself to proclaiming the greatness of God. It should be no wonder that God empowered his preaching as He did.

---

30. Ibid.

CHAPTER SEVEN

Doctrinally Grounded

There was nothing that interested Martyn Lloyd-Jones more than theology. It was his absorbing passion and the key to the understanding not only of his mental and intellectual preferences, but also to the manner both of his preaching and of his living.[1]

—PHILIP EDGCUMBE HUGHES

From the beginning of his ministry, Martyn Lloyd-Jones was committed to the kind of expository preaching that he described as "theology on fire."[2] He was adamant that true preaching must be doctrinal preaching. Lloyd-Jones asked, "What is preaching?" He answered, "It is theology on fire. And a theology which does not take fire, I maintain, is a defective theology; or at least the man's understanding of it is defective.

---

1. Philip Edgcumbe Hughes, "The Theologian," in Catherwood, *Chosen by God*, 162.
2. Lloyd-Jones, *Preaching and Preachers*, 97.

Preaching is theology coming through a man who is on fire."[3] Each sermon, he maintained, must set forth specific doctrinal truths that are presented in a text of Scripture. Simply put, biblical preaching must be exposition that is theologically grounded.

To this point, Lloyd-Jones asserted: "Preaching must always be theological, always based on a theological foundation. . . . There is no type of preaching that should be non-theological."[4] With compelling insight, he explained: "You cannot deal properly with repentance without dealing with the doctrine of man, the doctrine of the Fall, the doctrine of sin and the wrath of God against sin."[5] Each doctrine in Scripture is inseparably joined to every other doctrine. Preaching must be aimed at teaching what he called "doctrinal certainties"[6] that unify the entire Bible in one cohesive body of truth.

Lloyd-Jones did not arrive at these theological convictions independent of outside help. He was greatly influenced by the Puritans—who, unlike their critics, he actually read. He read all of Richard Baxter's *Christian Directory* and many volumes of John Owen. The spirit of Puritanism, Lloyd-Jones believed, could be traced from William Tyndale to John Knox to John Owen to Charles Spurgeon. It was this spirit of the centrality of God's Word that drove this preacher from Wales.

Lloyd-Jones' theological framework was also greatly shaped

---

3. Ibid.

4. Ibid., 64-65.

5. Ibid.

6. Iain H. Murray, *John MacArthur: Servant of the Word and Flock* (Edinburgh, Scotland: Banner of Truth, 2011), 28.

by the American Colonial pastor Jonathan Edwards. One day early in 1929, Lloyd-Jones had time to spare as he waited for a train in Cardiff, so he visited the secondhand bookshop of John Evans. "There," he said, "down on my knees in my overcoat in the corner of the shop, I found the two-volume 1834 edition of Edwards which I bought for five shillings. I devoured these volumes and literally just read and read them. It is certainly true that they helped me more than anything else."[7] In the following years, Lloyd-Jones turned to Edwards for instruction and edification again and again. He even encouraged young preachers to read and study the words of Edwards:

> I can simply testify that in my experience the help that I derived in my early years in the ministry from reading the sermons of Jonathan Edwards was immeasurable. And, of course not only his sermons, but also his account of that Great Awakening, that great religious Revival that took place in America in the eighteenth century, and his great *The Religious Affections*. All that was invaluable because Edwards was an expert in dealing with the states and conditions of the soul. He dealt in a very practical manner with problems arising in a pastoral ministry among people who were passing through the various phases of spiritual experience. This is invaluable to the preacher.[8]

---

7. Murray, *The First Forty Years*, 253–54.
8. Lloyd-Jones, *Preaching and Preachers*, 176.

Lloyd-Jones believed Edwards to have the most relevant message to the present condition of Christianity. Edwards especially influenced Lloyd-Jones' view of revival. Edwards was "preeminently the theologian of revival, the theologian of experience, or as some have put it 'the theologian of the heart.'"[9] What encouraged Lloyd-Jones regarding Edwards was his "mighty intellect," paired with his unparalleled knowledge of "the workings of the human heart, regenerate and unregenerate."[10] Edwards was "unique," "superlative" and "preeminently the expert" in his analysis of individual and communal spiritual experience. "If you want to know anything about revival," Lloyd-Jones insisted, "Edwards is the man to consult. His knowledge of the human heart, and the psychology of human nature, is quite incomparable."[11]

Quite naturally, Lloyd-Jones drew parallels between Edwardsian thought and experience and Welsh Calvinistic Methodism. One parallel concerned a new hymnbook by William Williams that came out in Wales in 1763; Lloyd-Jones noted that "as the people began to sing these great expressions of theology a revival broke out."[12] What was significant about Williams, as a hymn-writer who stimulated revival, was that he combined the great theological themes taken up and versified by Isaac Watts with the rich

---

9. Lloyd-Jones, *The Puritans*, 361.
10. Ibid.
11. Ibid.
12. Ibid., 202–3.

experience to be found in the hymns of Charles Wesley. According to Lloyd-Jones, this combination was part of the genius of Calvinistic Methodism. Lloyd-Jones argued that Welsh Calvinistic Methodism was not merely a continuation of Puritanism, but the new element was "the revival aspect." In light of this, Lloyd-Jones suggested that "Jonathan Edwards must be called a Calvinistic Methodist."[13] Whether Edwards would have categorized himself in this manner is not particularly the point. What mattered was that for Edwards—who for Lloyd-Jones was the dean of theological thinkers—religion was that which "belongs essentially to the heart."[14]

As a result of the influence of the Puritans, Edwards, and others, the Doctor's doctrinal stance was shaped into a robust biblical theology that was full of zeal and passion for the gospel. This fire ignited his preaching and shaped how he viewed preaching. Theology, for Lloyd-Jones, was the match that lit the flame in the pulpit.

The Backbone of Preaching

Consequently, Lloyd-Jones understood that biblical preaching necessitates that the preacher have a strategic grasp of systematic theology: "To me there is nothing more important in a

---

13. Ibid., 205.
14. Ibid., 357.

preacher than that he should know it and be well grounded in it. This systematic theology, this body of truth which is derived from the Scripture, should always be present as a background and as a controlling influence in his preaching."[15] For Lloyd-Jones, the theology that runs through the entire Bible forms the very backbone of Scripture. Therefore, it must be the spine of his preaching. He knew that each individual passage he expounded must be tested by the analogy of Scripture—that is, its teaching must be in alignment with what the rest of Scripture teaches.

Iain H. Murray explains in his biography that Lloyd-Jones saw the purpose of expositional preaching as "not simply to give the correct grammatical sense of a verse or passage. It is rather to set out the principles or doctrines which the words are intended to convey. True expository preaching is, therefore, doctrinal preaching, it is preaching which addresses specific truths from God to man."[16] When a preacher does not teach the doctrine in a passage, his sermon fails to channel the divine power toward the listener. Thus, Lloyd-Jones asserted, "The purpose of studying the Scripture is to arrive at doctrine."[17] Setting forth the theology of the passage, Lloyd-Jones maintained, is essential to achieving the desired effect of the sermon.

---

15. Lloyd-Jones, *Preaching and Preachers*, 66.

16. Murray, *The Life of Martyn Lloyd-Jones*, 261.

17. D. Martyn Lloyd-Jones, *Faith on Trial* (Clover, S.C.: Christian Heritage, 2008), 88.

The Modern Aversion to Theology

Lloyd-Jones recognized that despite the necessity of theology in preaching, there existed a resistance to it in the modern church. He stated:

> We live in an age in which we do not hear very much about doctrines, and there are some people who are even foolish enough to say that they do not like them, which seems to me to be a very pathetic and regrettable attitude. Lectures or sermons on biblical doctrines were once very common but they have become comparatively uncommon, especially during this century.[18]

The Doctor lamented the confusion in the church regarding its beliefs. He stressed, "There is an absence of doctrine, there is a lack of clear definition and a readiness to allow anybody to say anything they like."[19] To reverse this decline, Lloyd-Jones asserted:

> This means that there was never a time when it was more urgently necessary that Christian people should consider together the doctrines of the Bible. We must know the ground on which we stand, and be able to withstand every enemy that comes to attack us, every

---

18. *The Christ-Centered Preaching of Martyn Lloyd-Jones*, 107.
19. Lloyd-Jones, *Great Doctrines*, 9.

subtle foe, every ploy used by the devil who comes disguised as an "angel of light" to ruin our souls.[20]

Iain Murray writes, "He came to see the failure of evangelicals to recognize the importance of doctrine as a besetting weakness."[21] This is how Lloyd-Jones came to see the church in the time before World War II:

Precise thinking, and definition, and dogma have been at a serious discount. The whole emphasis has been placed upon religion as a power which can do things for us and make us happy. The emotional and feeling side of religion has been over-emphasised at the expense of the intellectual. Far too often people have thought of it [the Christian religion] merely as something that gives a constant series of miraculous deliverances from all sorts and kinds of ills. . . . The impression has often been given that we have but to ask God for whatever we may chance to need and we shall be satisfied. . . . The great principles, the mighty background, the intellectual and theological content of our faith have not been emphasized, and indeed, oftentimes, have been dismissed as non-essentials.[22]

---

20. Ibid.

21. Iain H. Murray, *Lloyd-Jones: Messenger of Grace* (Edinburgh, Scotland: Banner of Truth, 2008), 229.

22. Martyn Lloyd-Jones, *Why Does God Allow War?* (Wheaton, Ill.: Crossway, 2003), 45–46.

Returning to Sound Doctrine

The congregation must be taught sound doctrine from the pulpit, Lloyd-Jones believed. Otherwise, they will be susceptible to serious error. Lloyd-Jones said: "It is not enough merely to give people an open Bible. Perfectly sincere and genuine and able men and women may read this book and say things that are quite wrong. We must define our doctrines."[23]

From the very beginning of his ministry, the Doctor was unashamedly committed to the faithful teaching of theology. He stated, "To read my Bible properly means that I must consider doctrine."[24] He believed that doctrinal truths must be preached in order to rightly exposit the Scripture. Concerning the preaching of the Apostles, he stated, "Their way of preaching was to proclaim doctrine."[25]

Lloyd-Jones believed that exposition should contain the kind of high theology that magnifies the glory of God. He said, "It is our business to face the Scriptures. One advantage in preaching through a book of the Bible, as we are proposing to do, is that it compels us to face every single statement, come what may, and stand before it, and look at it, and allow it to speak to us."[26] He believed that any careful, Spirit-illumined study of the Bible reveals theological truths that must be preached.

---

23. Lloyd-Jones, *Great Doctrines*, 8.
24. Ibid., 7.
25. Ibid.
26. Lloyd-Jones, *God's Ultimate Purpose*, 84.

Lloyd-Jones firmly believed that true preaching requires that the doctrinal truths in a text must be expounded. He stated: "Great preaching always depends upon great themes. Great themes always produce great speaking in any realm, and this is particularly true, of course, in the realm of the Church. While men believed in the Scriptures as the authoritative Word of God and spoke on the basis of that authority you had great preaching."[27] However, when the church abandoned theological certainty, the pulpit immediately lost its power. He explained:

> But once that went, and men began to speculate, and to theorize, and to put up hypotheses and so on, the eloquence and the greatness of the spoken word inevitably declined and began to wane. You cannot really deal with speculations and conjectures in the same way as preaching had formerly dealt with the great themes of the Scriptures. But as belief in the great doctrines of the Bible began to go out, and sermons were replaced by ethical addresses and homilies, and moral uplift and sociopolitical talk, it is not surprising that preaching declined. I suggest that this is the first and the greatest cause of this decline.[28]

---

27. Lloyd-Jones, *Preaching and Preachers*, 13.
28. Ibid.

If the church is to be strong, Lloyd-Jones believed the preacher must deliver the comprehensive theology of the Bible. This is what he believed Paul meant by "the full counsel of God" (Acts 20:27). He stressed, "The preacher should be well-versed in biblical theology which in turn leads on to a systematic theology . . . this body of truth which is derived from the Scripture, should always be present as a background and as a controlling influence in his preaching."[29] As a physician must know medicine, he believed, a preacher must know sound doctrine. Lloyd-Jones was one who was well-versed in systematic theology, and this knowledge gave accuracy and power to his preaching.

As Lloyd-Jones expounded a passage, he never did so in a cold, clinical fashion. Theology should always ignite the heart, both in the preacher and the listener. Theology must be the foundation of every sermon. He explained, "When you call men to come to Christ and to give themselves to Him, how can you do so without knowing who He is, and on what grounds you invite them to come to Him, and so on. In other words it is all highly theological."[30]

Lloyd-Jones also underscored the importance of biblical theology, which is the basis of systematic theology. He continued, "The preacher should be well versed in biblical theology which in turn leads on to a systematic theology."[31]

---

29. Ibid., 66.
30. Ibid., 64–65.
31. Ibid., 66.

The expositor must know the theological framework of the entire Bible. For Lloyd-Jones, each truth of theology is like a link in a chain that runs through all of Scripture. He said:

> The doctrine in a particular text, we must always remember, is a part of this greater whole—the Truth or the Faith. That is the meaning of the phrase "comparing Scripture with Scripture." We must not deal with any text in isolation; all our preparation of a sermon should be controlled by this background of systematic theology.[32]

What separated Lloyd-Jones from most preachers of his day was this focus upon doctrinal truth. This was also the main distinction between Lloyd-Jones and his predecessor at Westminster Chapel, G. Campbell Morgan. The elder preacher was much more devotional, preferring to deliver general observations and niceties in his preaching, where Lloyd-Jones gave greater attention to theology. However, Lloyd-Jones firmly believed, "Exposition needs to lead hearers to doctrinal certainties."[33] Consequently, he was committed to preaching sound theology from each passage before him.

---

32. Ibid.
33. Murray, *John MacArthur*, 28.

THE FOUNDATION OF HIS THEOLOGY

Doctrinal preaching was a part of Lloyd-Jones' upbringing. He had been a member of the Welsh Calvinistic Methodist Church, first in Wales and then in London. His theology was influenced by the "experiential Calvinism" of the English and American Puritans, which made him an heir to the great Calvinistic preachers of previous generations. Murray notes: "When people sought to explain what set Lloyd-Jones apart in terms of his convictions they usually did so in terms of 'Calvinism.' "[34] When once asked what made his preaching so different from the preaching of others, Lloyd-Jones replied that he had read different books. He meant that he had deliberately immersed himself in the writings of the Reformed-minded Puritans, who were theologically precise in their handling of Scripture.

In a lecture at Westminster Theological Seminary, he confessed that his whole ministry had been governed by the works of the Puritans.[35] Added to this influence was Lloyd-Jones' indebtedness to the eighteenth-century Evangelical Revival in Wales, England, and Scotland. He considered himself to be an "eighteenth-century man" who lived in a different world. He stated:

> I draw a great distinction between the preaching of the
> Puritans and the preaching of the eighteenth-century

---

34. Murray, *The Fight of Faith*, 193.
35. Lloyd-Jones, *The Puritans*, 152.

men. I myself am an eighteenth-century man, not seventeenth-century; but I believe in using the seventeenth-century men as the eighteenth-century men used them.[36]

Here, Lloyd-Jones meant that he embraced the Reformed theology of the Puritans in the seventeenth century, but when he preached, he did so in the fiery manner of those leaders in the Great Awakening in the Colonies and the Evangelical Awakening in Britain in the eighteenth century. Thus, we make a mistake if we try to explain Lloyd-Jones' evangelistic preaching only by making a comparison with the Puritans. He saw the Puritans mainly through the eyes of the men of the Evangelical Revival.

The examples of George Whitefield, John and Charles Wesley, Daniel Rowland, and Howell Harris were much more significant for Lloyd-Jones than were the Puritans themselves.[37] He was born in an area of Wales where Calvinistic Methodism had a powerful influence in igniting the Evangelical Revival. The village of Llangeitho, where Lloyd-Jones grew up, had a statue of Daniel Rowland near the Calvinistic Methodist Chapel. When Lloyd-Jones was minister of the Calvinistic Methodist church in Aberavon, he organized

---

36. Lloyd-Jones, *Preaching and Preachers*, 120.
37. A large percentage of his lectures on the yearly Puritan and Westminster Conferences were not directly on the Puritans but on eighteenth-century men who had been influenced by the Puritans (e.g. George Whitefield, Howell Harris, William Williams). See Lloyd-Jones, *The Puritans*.

excursions for men in his church to visit this statue and other spots of the Welsh Methodist awakening. His hope was to see another revival birthed in the flames of similar preaching. Lloyd-Jones patterned his pulpit ministry after these itinerant Calvinistic Methodist preachers.

The influence of these Calvinistic Methodist preachers began when Lloyd-Jones was still a teenager and his history teacher thrust a booklet into his pocket. It was about the ministry of Howell Harris, the great Welsh evangelist of the eighteenth century. This book eventually contributed to his conversion, but beyond that, it impressed a strong vision upon his heart about what evangelical preaching should look like. Throughout his ministry, the theology and methodology of these early Calvinistic Methodists remained for him the standard for proclaiming the Word of God.

FACING THE SCRIPTURE

The advice of Lloyd-Jones to preachers is this: "Our primary call is to deliver this whole message, this 'whole counsel of God.'"[38] He believed the preacher must be firmly committed to a thorough theological understanding of Scripture in order to proclaim God. He felt the preacher should be knowledgeable of the tenets of theology. Therefore, theology was the firm foundation of his preaching. He stated:

---

38. Lloyd-Jones, *Preaching and Preachers*, 67.

> The doctrines of the Bible are not a subject to be studied; rather we should desire to know them in order that, having known them, we may not be "puffed up" with knowledge, and excited about our information, but may draw nearer to God in worship, praise, and adoration, because we have seen, in a fuller way than we have ever seen before, the glory of our wondrous God.[39]

Lloyd-Jones did not see theology as an end to itself. Rather, the end of theology is the vastness and wonder of God. Expositors should study theology to know God that they may be lost in wonder, love, and praise. Theology, for the Doctor, is never cold, dry, and callous. It is vibrant, life-changing, and transformative when proclaimed in the authority of Scripture. Let us study theology to know God and so that others may come to know Him better.

---

39. Lloyd-Jones, *Great Doctrines,* 10.

CHAPTER EIGHT

Theologically Reformed

D. Martyn Lloyd-Jones was one of the most formative figures of twentieth-century, English-speaking Evangelicalism. . . . His robust grasp of what has been termed the doctrines of grace, his passion for the great displays of God's glory in the past—particularly in the Age of Revival, the eighteenth century—and his remarkable preaching made him critical to the recovery and spread of evangelical, experiential Calvinism.[1]

—MICHAEL A.G. HAYKIN

In terms of doctrine, the biblical expositions of Lloyd-Jones were distinctly Reformed. Many would identify them as Calvinistic. One needs to look no further than his Friday-evening studies on the great doctrines of the Bible and on Romans to see his fundamental commitment to the Reformed understanding of Scripture. The same can be said

---

1. Michael A.G. Haykin, "From the Editor," *Eusebeia* 7 (Spring 2007): 3.

of his Sunday-morning sermons on Ephesians. Here, one can easily discover the real depth and strength of his pulpit ministry. To this end, Iain Murray writes: "When people try to explain what set Martyn Lloyd-Jones apart in terms of his convictions they usually did so in terms of 'Calvinism.' . . . Dr. Lloyd-Jones believed that a restoration of the standpoint which is called Calvinistic was a fundamental need."[2] Murray explains: "It was needed because it was biblical; because it shows how the gospel begins not with man and his happiness but with God and His glory."[3]

Whatever was biblical, Lloyd-Jones believed. Moreover, whatever he believed, he preached. This meant the exposition of all the robust distinctives of biblical Calvinism. However, it is important to point out that "in all of his sermons," Murray said, "nothing will be found with a title such as 'The Five Points of Calvinism.'"[4] Instead of labeling the doctrine he was preaching, Lloyd-Jones opted to simply explain the text of Scripture. Murray comments, "He believed that the best way of presenting doctrine is to teach the *text* of Scripture; the preacher's concern should not be that people take up a name or label, but that they gain a spiritual understanding of the word of God."[5] Anyone who heard his doctrinally rich sermons would be able to recognize the Calvinistic nuance of his theology, but he chose not to label it as such while in the pulpit.

---

2. Murray, *The Fight of Faith*, 193.

3. Ibid.

4. Murray, *Messenger of Grace*, 232.

5. Ibid.

While the Doctor believed in the doctrines of grace, it is necessary to emphasize that he did not believe each of the five points should have equal prominence.[6] For instance, according to Murray, "In the case of preaching to unbelievers, he did not think that some of the Points warranted prominence at all."[7] While engaged in evangelistic preaching to unbelievers, Lloyd-Jones strongly emphasized the doctrine of total depravity but never followed that with the doctrine of unconditional election. He thought to do so was quite wrong. He believed affirmation of the five points of Calvinism would come later as people came to faith in Christ and grew in their knowledge of God's Word. Belief in the five points is not a prerequisite for salvation. The only requirement to be saved is to recognize one's sinful condition and the need to cling to Christ by faith as one's only hope of justification.

While Lloyd-Jones did not employ the use of labels in the pulpit to explain theology or doctrine, he nevertheless affirmed his belief and acceptance of the doctrines of grace as taught in Scripture. In a radio address for the BBC in Wales on June 25, 1944, Lloyd-Jones addressed the God-centered theology of the great Genevan Reformer John Calvin:

> Calvin's main feature is that he bases everything on the Bible. . . . He does not wish for any philosophy apart

---

6. Ibid.
7. Ibid.

from that which emanates from the Scripture. . . . For him the great central and all-important truth was the sovereignty of God and God's glory. We must start here and everything else issues from here. It was God, of His own free will and according to His infinite wisdom, who created the world. . . . Everyone would be lost if God had not elected some for salvation and that unconditionally. It is only through Christ's death that it is possible for these people to be saved, and they would not see or accept that salvation if God through His irresistible grace in the Holy Spirit had not opened their eyes and persuaded them to accept the offer. And even after that, it is God who sustains them and keeps them from falling. Their salvation, therefore, is sure because it depends, not on them and their ability, but on God's grace.[8]

Calvin understood that the doctrines of sovereign grace bring the greatest glory to God, a conviction that Lloyd-Jones shared: "The whole purpose of your salvation and mine is that we should glorify the Father. Oh, that we might grasp this! . . . The ultimate aim and object of our salvation is that we may glorify God."[9] These truths must be preached because they magnify God and humble man. Simply put, Lloyd-Jones

---

8. Lloyd-Jones, *Knowing the Times*, 35–36.
9. D. Martyn Lloyd-Jones, *The Assurance of Our Salvation: Exploring the Depth of Jesus' Prayer for His Own; Studies in John 17* (Wheaton, Ill.: Crossway, 2000), 46–47.

preached these great doctrines because they spread the fame of the divine name.

These God-centered truths empowered his preaching and fueled his evangelistic fervor. In order to understand the dynamic of his pulpit, it is critical to grasp his strategic hold on these biblical truths.

TOTAL DEPRAVITY

Lloyd-Jones affirmed the foundational doctrine of total depravity, also known as radical corruption. He understood that before an expositor can communicate the good news of God's salvation, he first must convey the bad news of man's condemnation. The black velvet backdrop of man's sin must be laid out before the sparkling diamond of God's sovereign grace can be seen in its dazzling luster. Lloyd-Jones held to this doctrine so firmly that he believed that no one could rightly understand the grace of God without it. He said, "No man will ever have a true conception of the biblical teaching of redemption if he is not clear about the biblical doctrine of sin."[10]

The doctrine of total depravity begins with the teaching on Adam's original sin, the act of disobedience that brought death to the human race. When the first couple ate the forbidden fruit from the tree, sin immediately separated them from God. Guilt pervaded their entire nature:

---

10. D. Martyn Lloyd-Jones, *God's Way of Reconciliation* (Grand Rapids, Mich.: Baker, 1972), 14.

The first thing we are told is that Adam and Eve became conscious of their flesh (Genesis 3:7). This is an extraordinary thing. Man, as he was made originally by God, was quite unselfconscious about his body (Genesis 2:25). The man and the woman were naked, and that was no trouble to them at all. But the moment they sinned, the moment they fell, shame developed and they tried to cover themselves with fig leaves.[11]

As a result of this transgression, sin was imputed to the entire human race. This original sin rendered all men guilty under divine judgment. Lloyd-Jones explained, "When Adam committed that one sin, though we had not committed it, it was imputed to us all."[12] The fall of Adam resulted in the condemnation of the entire human race.

Moreover, Lloyd-Jones held that all people are born with a sin-corrupted nature. Depravity has spread to their entire being. The mind of man is blinded, his heart is bankrupt, his will is bound. He commented:

Why is it that man ever chooses to sin? The answer is that man has fallen away from God, and as a result, his whole nature has become perverted and sinful. Man's whole bias is away from God. By nature, he hates God and feels that God is opposed to him. His

11. Lloyd-Jones, *Great Doctrines*, 185.
12. Ibid., 198.

144

god is himself, his own abilities and powers, his own desires. He objects to the whole idea of God and the demands, which God makes upon him. . . . Furthermore, man likes and covets the things that God prohibits, and dislikes the things and the kind of life to which God calls him. These are no mere dogmatic statements. They are facts. . . . They alone explain the moral muddle and the ugliness that characterize life to such an extent today.[13]

In the view of Lloyd-Jones, this is the only proper explanation for the devastation of the world. The real problem of mankind is not his need for a better environment. Neither is it the need to solve man's social, political, or financial deficiencies. The trouble in the world, he taught, is the spiritual bankruptcy of the human race. He stated:

You cannot understand life as it is in this world at this moment unless you understand this biblical doctrine of sin. I go further: I suggest that you cannot understand the whole of human history apart from this, with all its wars and its quarrels and its conquests, its calamities, and all that it records. I assert that there is no adequate explanation save in the biblical doctrine of sin. The history of the world can only

---

13. D. Martyn Lloyd-Jones, *The Plight of Man and the Power of God* (Grand Rapids, Mich.: Eerdmans, 1945), 87.

be understood truly in the light of this great biblical doctrine of man, fallen and in sin.[14]

Lloyd-Jones affirmed that man, by his fallen nature, is lost and utterly depraved. He is plagued by moral inability and is unable to save himself or live in a manner pleasing to God. Being dead in sin, no person can earn a favorable standing before God.

UNCONDITIONAL ELECTION

Lloyd-Jones proclaimed the doctrine of unconditional election. This biblical truth is inseparably connected with the teaching of human depravity. Because his will is spiritually dead and bound by moral inability, man cannot choose God. Therefore, if anyone is to be rescued from perishing, God must exercise His sovereign will to save. Out of the mass of fallen humanity, Lloyd-Jones asserted that God made a distinguishing choice among all people. Before the foundation of the world, He sovereignly determined a people whom He would save. He maintained, "The church is a collection of the elect."[15] Were it not for God's eternal choice of some, none would be saved.

Expounding Romans 9:10–13, Lloyd-Jones presented the biblical case that God has chosen a specific people by Himself and for Himself to save. He declared:

---

14. Lloyd-Jones, *God's Way of Reconciliation*, 15.
15. Lloyd-Jones, *Knowing the Times*, 35.

God brings His purpose to pass and carries it out by means of this process of selection and election for one reason only—because it is the only way which guarantees that His purpose and His plan will certainly and surely and infallibly be carried out and brought to a final fruition: "that the purpose of God according to election might stand." It does not depend upon us at all, but upon God Himself, His character and His action.[16]

In the pulpit, Lloyd-Jones preached that the eternal choice of God was not based upon any person's intrinsic merit, good works, or foreseen faith. Any autonomous act of saving faith on man's part is impossible as a result of radical corruption. The total depravity of man makes necessary God's sovereign choice to save whom He wills to save:

Man by nature rebels against God. He does so as the result of the Fall. Having listened to the suggestion of the devil and having fallen away from God, he is under "the wrath of God." How is it that any individual person has ever come out of that morass? The answer is that God has chosen such a person to be delivered from it unto salvation."[17]

---

16. D. Martyn Lloyd-Jones, *Romans: Exposition of Chapter 9; God's Sovereign Purpose* (Edinburgh, Scotland: Banner of Truth, 1991), 129.

17. Lloyd-Jones, *God's Ultimate Purpose*, 83.

Lloyd-Jones believed that all those chosen by God are elected solely by God's good pleasure and nothing else: "We are chosen by God simply as the result of His own good pleasure, or, to use scriptural phraseology, 'according to the good pleasure of His will,' and entirely apart from anything we have ever done or said or thought."[18] Again, he states, "We are chosen by God out of the good pleasure of His own will in spite of ourselves, in spite of the fact that we were enemies, aliens, and even haters of God."[19] In the book of Ephesians, this is why "Paul puts [the doctrine of election] first in order to show how we become Christians."[20]

In understanding the truth of sovereign election, Lloyd-Jones believed that many other doctrines are clearly seen: "It is in the light of this doctrine that we see the certainty of the plan of salvation most clearly. If God's plan of salvation were to be dependent upon man, and the choice of man, it would certainly fail; but if it is of God from beginning to end, then it is certain."[21]

By this truth of election, Lloyd-Jones saw that all grace comes by divine initiative: "It was God's hand that laid hold of me, and drew me out, and separated me. . . . I am what I am because of God's grace; and I give to Him all the glory. Were I to believe that my future is dependent upon myself

18. Ibid.
19. Ibid.
20. Ibid., 92.
21. Ibid.

and my decisions I would tremble in fear; but I thank God that I know that I am in His hand."[22] God's sovereign choice of certain individuals took place in eternity past: "I know that before time began, before the foundation of the world, He looked at me and saw me and selected me, and in His mind gave me to Christ."[23]

In a sermon on Ephesians 1:4, Lloyd-Jones argued that belief in the divine sovereignty of election does not negate the work of evangelism in the pulpit. Rather, it necessitates our involvement in preaching the gospel. To explain, he used the illustration of the farmer who must sow his seed before God will cause it to germinate and bring forth life. In like manner, the preacher must sow the good seed of the Word before God will cause it to take root in the hearts of the elect. He explained:

> People often argue that this doctrine of divine election and choice leaves no place for evangelism, for preaching the gospel, for urging people to repent and to believe, and for the use of arguments and persuasions in doing so. But there is no contradiction here any more than there is in saying that since it is God that gives us the crops of corn in the autumn, therefore the farmer need not plough and harrow and sow; the answer to which is that God has ordained both. God

---

22. Ibid.
23. Ibid.

has chosen to call out His people by means of evangelism and the preaching of the Word. He ordains the
means as well as the end.[24]

The doctrine of sovereign election gave Lloyd-Jones
great confidence in carrying out the work of evangelism in
his gospel preaching. He realized that the biblical teaching of
election guaranteed the success of his gospel preaching. This
truth never dampened his evangelistic efforts in the pulpit but
emboldened them.

DEFINITE ATONEMENT

Lloyd-Jones espoused the doctrine of definite atonement. This
truth teaches that Christ died exclusively and effectually for
those chosen by the Father. On the cross, He did not merely
make it possible for mankind to be saved but actually secured
the salvation of all those for whom He died. This Reformed
doctrine ignited his soul and fueled his preaching.

This position, also known as particular redemption,
stands in contrast to the Arminian view that Christ did not
actually save anyone in particular by His death, but merely
made salvation available to everyone. Lloyd-Jones emphati-
cally rejected this aberrant view of a universal atonement. In a
sermon on Ephesians 5:25, he articulated that Christ "died for
the church. He died for nobody else." Preaching on Romans

---

24. Ibid., 90.

3:25, Lloyd-Jones affirmed that saving grace in Christ at the cross was secured only for those who place saving faith in Him as Savior and Lord. Christ's death on the cross was for only those who put their faith in Him:

> His life was poured out in death. He is the Lamb of God. He is our Substitute. He died for us, and for our sins. "By His stripes we are healed." Of whom is this true? It is true of all—and of them alone—who have faith in Him, "whom God hath set forth to be a propitiation through faith in His blood." This does not cover everybody; this only applies to those who have faith in Him. . . . This grand atonement is ours and becomes ours only by faith.[25]

Lloyd-Jones was unmistakably clear that those who believe in Christ are the ones for whom Christ died. It was for these alone that Christ died. In a sermon from Romans 8:28–30, Lloyd-Jones further affirmed this truth:

> We must understand and realize that God's whole purpose in sending His only begotten Son into this world was to ensure that His plan of salvation could not fail. It cannot go wrong or fall short in any respect. God has chosen the people whom He has given to His Son;

---

25. D. Martyn Lloyd-Jones, *Romans: Exposition of Chapter 3:20–4:25; Atonement and Justification* (Edinburgh, Scotland: Banner of Truth, 1970), 93.

and the Son has said that He came into the world to do this work for them at the behest of His Father. It cannot fail; otherwise the glory of God would not be vindicated, and the devil would still be triumphant.[26]

From this statement, it is clear that Lloyd-Jones preached the doctrine of particular redemption. Christ died for all the elect. If He had died for the non-elect also, Lloyd-Jones reasoned, the devil would triumph over the work of the cross.

For Lloyd-Jones, the cross is the heart of the gospel. Preaching on John 17:10, Lloyd-Jones proclaimed:

The cross is the only thing in which we should glory; I recognize what is happening there and I know that the Son of God has come down to earth and has come down to that cross, in order that I might be forgiven and that I might be made a child of God. In believing in Him in this way I glorify Him, and it is my desire that I should do so.[27]

Lloyd-Jones' view of the atonement was in stark contrast to many in his day. This includes R.T. Kendall, who followed Lloyd-Jones as minister of Westminster Chapel in 1977.

---

26. D. Martyn Lloyd-Jones, *Romans: The Perseverance of the Saints; Exposition of Chapter 8:17–39* (Grand Rapids, Mich.: Zondervan, 1975), 361.

27. Lloyd-Jones, *The Assurance of Salvation*, 274.

Kendall held that Calvin and Lloyd-Jones taught universal redemption. Iain Murray rebuts this assertion by stating that Lloyd-Jones remained silent on this issue in order not to create a controversy for his successor. Murray writes: "Martyn Lloyd-Jones was against any public controversy. Although he personally believed firmly in a definite not a universal atonement."[28] Murray adds, "The last thing he wanted was disunity among men who otherwise appeared to hold Calvinistic beliefs in common."[29] Nevertheless, Lloyd-Jones held firmly to the biblical doctrine of a particular redemption.

IRRESISTIBLE GRACE

Lloyd-Jones endorsed the doctrine of irresistible grace. This is the biblical teaching of the sovereign work of the Holy Spirit in convicting, calling, drawing, and regenerating elect sinners. This effectual work grants saving faith to those chosen by the Father and purchased by the Son. Those whom the Father elected in eternity past and for whom the Son died are those whom the Spirit brings to faith in Jesus Christ. None whom the Father elected and for whom Christ died will fail to believe and be born again. The Holy Spirit guarantees this by granting repentance and faith to these elect ones in order to ensure their conversion to Christ.

---

28. Murray, *The Life of Martyn Lloyd-Jones*, 723.
29. Ibid.

Summarizing the biblical teaching of this irresistible call, Lloyd-Jones stated:

> Man is a fallen creature, with his mind in a state of enmity towards God. He is totally unable to save himself and to reunite himself with God. Everyone would be lost if God had not elected some for salvation and that unconditionally. It is only through Christ's death that it is possible for these people to be saved, and they would not see or accept that salvation if God through His irresistible grace in the Holy Spirit had not opened their eyes and persuaded them (not forced them) to accept that offer.[30]

The effectual calling of the Holy Spirit includes the doctrine of regeneration. In July 1951, the Doctor gave three addresses on the sovereignty of God at the third InterVarsity Fellowship Welsh Conference at Pantyfedwen, Borth. In the third address, he said the doctrine of unconditional election is inseparably connected to the doctrine of regeneration:

> Some people will persist in discussing election apart from regeneration, but the truth about regeneration is vital and essential to the whole doctrine of sovereignty. When a man becomes a Christian he is a new creature, he is born again. The natural man is not

---

30. Lloyd-Jones, *Knowing the Times*, 35.

regenerate. He is an enemy and an alien in relation to God. He cannot see these truths. If he had the capacity to see them, he would not need to be regenerate. We must think of man's condition in terms of life and death.[31]

In other words, Lloyd-Jones is clear that the natural man is spiritually dead. Without the regenerating power of the Holy Spirit, there is nothing in the sinner that can enable him to call upon Christ. The unregenerate's moral inability to believe upon Christ is what makes the effectual call of God so vital. Only through the Holy Spirit's work can those who are hopelessly lost be born again and believe in Christ. Lloyd-Jones clarified:

It is the internal operation of the Holy Spirit upon the soul and the heart of men and women that brings them into a condition in which the call can become effectual. And when the Spirit does it, of course, it is absolutely certain. . . . The Holy Spirit implants a principle within me which enables me, for the first time in my life, to discern and to apprehend something of this glorious, wondrous truth. He works upon my will. "It is God that worketh in you both to will and to do." He does not strike me; He does not beat me; He does not coerce me. No, thank God,

31. Murray, *The Life of Martyn Lloyd-Jones*, 243–44.

what He does is operate upon my will so that I desire these things and rejoice in them and love them. He leads, He persuades, He acts upon my will in such a way that when He does, the call of the gospel is effectual, and it is certain, and it is sure. God's work never fails, and when God works in a man or woman, the work is effective.[32]

Irresistible grace is not the coercion of the Spirit against man's will. Lloyd-Jones understood that the Spirit works to change the will of a person so that he desires to believe in Christ. God raises the spiritually dead sinner to new life and changes the inclination of the will. Suddenly, Christ becomes irresistible to this one, and he embraces Him by faith. This confidence in the powerful work of the Spirit gave impetus to Lloyd-Jones' commitment to evangelism and made his gospel preaching successful.

PRESERVING GRACE

Lloyd-Jones affirmed the doctrine of preserving grace, often known as the perseverance of the saints. This biblical truth teaches that no true believer in Christ will ever fall from grace. God upholds the faith of all who put their trust in Christ. Lloyd-Jones maintained, "It is God who sustains them and keeps them from falling. Their salvation, therefore, is sure

---

32. D. Martyn Lloyd-Jones, *God the Holy Spirit* (Wheaton, Ill.: Crossway, 1997), 73.

because it depends, not on them and their ability, but on God's grace."[33] It is not the believer's hold on Christ that keeps one saved but Christ's hold on the believer.

In a sermon on Romans 8:28–30, Lloyd-Jones affirmed that those who are genuine Christians cannot fall away from salvation. He proclaimed:

> We are not only forgiven, we are not merely believers; God has done these things to us. He has not only given us new life, He has "united" us to Christ; we are bound to Him by bonds that are indissoluble. Everything we are told about the true Christian makes it impossible for him to fall away. The only people who can fall away from the Church are those who are temporary believers, false professors, people with just an intellectual, temporary faith. But the man who is given new life, who is a "partaker of the divine nature" and who is "in Christ," by definition of terms cannot fall away.[34]

To say that a Christian can fall away and cease being a believer would be to misunderstand the comprehensive nature of the sovereign grace of God in salvation. In this same sermon, Lloyd-Jones maintained, "Everything we are told about the Christian, about the believer, carries with it this inevitable implication of 'the final perseverance of the saints.'"[35] To deny

---

33. Lloyd-Jones, *Knowing the Times*, 35.
34. Lloyd-Jones, *The Final Perseverance of the Saints*, 344.
35. Ibid., 345.

this truth of preserving grace, he contended, is to deny the very nature of grace itself.

Lloyd-Jones believed that assurance of salvation is not necessarily attained easily. Quite the contrary, assurance is something that comes to the one who is continually strengthened by the Holy Spirit throughout his Christian life. As their confidence in the love of God and their assurance of salvation grows, Christian men and women receive great courage during hardship and persecution, Lloyd-Jones affirmed:

> What was it that enabled men to do things like that, and to do things which were even more hazardous? It was that they believed in what is called the "Doctrine of the Perseverance of the Saints," it was because they had seen themselves in the plan of God which cannot be broken and which cannot fail. It is as absolute as God, Himself; He knows the end as well as the beginning. "Neither shall any man," said Christ, "pluck them out of my hand." It is unthinkable.[36]

This truth of preserving grace, Lloyd-Jones maintained, gives staying power to believers in the midst of their most difficult adversity. They are enabled to run the race set before them with endurance because they have great confidence in the fact that they are eternally upheld by God.

---

36. Lloyd-Jones, *The Assurance of Our Salvation*, 66.

CHAPTER NINE

Spiritually Empowered

Lloyd-Jones was one of the greatest preachers of his age . . . a man who spent a lifetime preaching and thinking about preaching.[1]

—J. LIGON DUNCAN III

As Martyn Lloyd-Jones stepped into the pulpit at West-minster Chapel, he bore the appearance of a man who was physically fragile and frail. He was short and had a small frame. His bald head, ringed with thin hair on the side, added to the appearance of weakness. In the eyes of the world, this was not a powerful individual who projected strength.

This is how the Doctor appeared to one visitor who came to Westminster Chapel during World War II. When this man

---

1. J. Ligon Duncan III, "Some Things to Look For and Wrestle With," in Lloyd-Jones, *Preaching and Preachers: 40th Anniversary Edition*, 33.

arrived, he found a note posted to the front door. It said that damage suffered from German bombings necessitated moving the worship service to a hall at another location. This individual walked to the temporary location and easily found a seat in a sparsely attended congregation.

As the service began, the visitor noted, "A small man in a collar and tie walked almost apologetically to the platform and called the people to worship. I remember thinking that Lloyd-Jones must be ill and that his place was being taken by one of his office-bearers."[2] This man standing before the people could not possibly be the preacher of note he had come to hear.

As the service continued, the first impression of the visitor remained unchanged. "This illusion [of weakness] was not dispelled during the first part of the service, though I was impressed by the quiet reverence of the man's prayers and his reading of the Bible."[3] Introverted and monotone, this man who was leading the service surely had to be a last-minute stand-in.

When it came time for the sermon, the same mild man stepped into the pulpit with a quiet demeanor: "Ultimately he announced his text and began his sermon in the same quiet voice."[4] As the sermon started, little changed. However, it is what followed that bears our notice. The visitor recounted:

---

2. Murray, *Messenger of Grace*, 30.

3. Ibid.

4. Ibid.

Then a curious thing happened. For the next forty minutes I became completely unconscious of everything except the word that this man was speaking—not his words, mark you, but someone behind them and in them and through them. I didn't realize it then, but I had been in the presence of the mystery of preaching, when a man is lost in the message he proclaims.[5]

This firsthand account could have been given by any one of countless individuals who heard the preaching of Martyn Lloyd-Jones. As was so often the case, the Doctor was captured by the power of God in his exposition. How could this man of slender figure and quiet demeanor be transformed into a powerhouse for God? There can be no explanation for this dramatic change apart from the dynamic activity of the Holy Spirit that controlled him.

Throughout his preaching ministry, Lloyd-Jones was consciously aware of his complete dependence upon the Holy Spirit to ensure the effectiveness of the sermon. His total reliance upon God was needed for divine illumination in his study and for supernatural energy in the pulpit. In his preparation, he knew the Holy Spirit had to be his Teacher, the One who would open his eyes and instruct him in the text. Moreover, the Spirit had to deepen his convictions in these truths. The same reliance was true in the role of the Spirit

---

5. Ibid.

in delivering the sermon. Lloyd-Jones believed there can be no real preaching apart from the internal empowering of the Spirit of God.

THE UNCTION OF THE HOLY SPIRIT

A world of difference exists, the Doctor believed, between being naturally gifted to deliver an address and being filled by the Spirit to preach the Word. He knew one can possess the natural ability to execute the work of preaching, but it is entirely something else to have the supernatural power to perform the assignment. Iain Murray observes this distinction as it existed in the mind of Lloyd-Jones:

> In his view, one could possess the natural ability and the understanding of the truth necessary to follow the expository method, and yet still never be a preacher at all. The Holy Spirit must be active in true preaching, active not only in owning the truth as it is heard, but active in anointing the preacher himself. Only then is his heart as well as his mind rightly engaged and the result is speech attended by liveliness, by unction and by the extemporaneous element already mentioned.[6]

---

6. Murray, *The Fight of Faith*, 262.

Explaining Lloyd-Jones' conviction, Murray notes: "True preaching does not belong to the sphere of natural gifts. It is not a thing to be obtained through teaching or training. It is the result of the presence of the Spirit of God."[7] This is why Lloyd-Jones strongly believed in the power of the Holy Spirit in the act of preaching. The Doctor said this work of the Spirit is "what is called in the New Testament 'unction'; He gives 'anointing,' understanding, "freedom and clarity of speech, an authority."[8] Further, he explained,

> What is meant by this "unction or anointing of the Spirit"? . . . What is this? It is the Holy Spirit falling upon the preacher in a special manner. It is an access of power. It is God giving power and enabling through the Spirit, to the preacher in order that he may do this work in a manner that lifts it up beyond the efforts and endeavors of man to a position in which the preacher is used by the Spirit and becomes a channel through whom the Spirit works. This is seen very plainly and clearly in the Scriptures.[9]

Lloyd-Jones argues both scripturally and historically for the unction of the Holy Spirit in preaching. True preaching,

---

7. Murray, *Messenger of Grace*, 31.
8. D. Martyn Lloyd-Jones, *Courageous Christianity* (Wheaton, Ill.: Crossway, 2001), 190–91.
9. Lloyd-Jones, *Preaching and Preachers*, 305.

he believed, finds its power in the mighty work of the Spirit. This is arguably the greatest need in the pulpit today.

STUDY MUST NOT BE NEGLECTED

To be clear, the Doctor did not believe the unction of the Spirit allowed the preacher to neglect his responsibility to study the Scriptures. To the contrary, he was convinced that the preacher must carefully prepare his sermon after a thorough investigation of the passage. He believed the Spirit is personally involved in the preacher's study just as He is when the preacher stands in the pulpit.

Lloyd-Jones added, "The right way to look upon the unction of the Spirit is to think of it as that which comes upon the preparation [of the sermon]. . . . Careful preparation, and the unction of the Holy Spirit, must never be regarded as alternatives but as complementary to each other."[10] The Spirit who authored the Scripture is the Spirit who must illumine the preacher's understanding of it. At the same time, the Spirit must enable the expositor to deliver these truths in the act of preaching. The Spirit must be present in each aspect of preaching, from the study to the pulpit.

Emphasizing this necessity, he used the example of the prophet Elijah at Mount Carmel. It was Elijah's responsibility to construct the altar, cut the wood, and place it upon the altar. He then had to kill the bull, cut it in pieces, and place it

---

10. Ibid.

on the wood. Then he prayed for fire to descend, and the fire fell. That, according to Lloyd-Jones, is the same order in the pulpit.[11] First, the preacher must do his part in sermon preparation. Then God must do His part in sending the fire. He commented, "The way to have power is to prepare your message carefully. Study the word of God, think it out, analyze it, put it in order, do your utmost. That is the message God is most likely to bless."[12] Lloyd-Jones believed God chooses to bless solid sermon preparation, not the lack of it.

Moreover, Lloyd-Jones used the examples of John the Baptist and the Apostles. He pointed out that though they were redeemed men, they still needed the empowerment of the Holy Spirit in order to carry out their preaching assignments. When expounding Acts 13:9, Lloyd-Jones noted that Paul needed to be filled with the Holy Spirit. He stated:

> When the record says there, "filled with the Holy Ghost," it is not referring back to the fact that he was filled with the Holy Ghost in connection with his conversion and as a result of his meeting with Ananias. It would be ridiculous to repeat this if it happened once and for all. This is again a special enduement of power, a special crisis, a special occasion, and he was given this special power for this special occasion.[13]

---

11. Ibid., 304.
12. D. Martyn Lloyd-Jones, *The Life of Peace* (Grand Rapids, Mich.: Baker, 1992), 225.
13. Lloyd-Jones, *Preaching and Preachers*, 310.

In an argument from the greater to the lesser, Lloyd-Jones reasoned if the Apostle Paul needed to be filled with the Spirit, then preachers who are less gifted need it much more.

From church history, Lloyd-Jones pointed out other examples of men who were filled by the Holy Spirit to preach the Word. He singled out Martin Luther as not only a great theologian, but an extraordinary preacher, because he was filled by the Spirit. He also added the examples of two lesser-known men. He referred to John Livingston, who in the power of the Spirit preached a sermon at Kirk O'Shotts in Scotland after which five hundred people were added to the churches. In addition, David Morgan, a mighty preacher in the Welsh revival of 1859, received a special unction of the Spirit and was empowered during this movement.

All preachers must be empowered by the Spirit, whether they be titanic figures like Luther or lesser-known individuals like Livingston and Morgan. Lloyd-Jones saw every preacher as in no less need of this same divine power.

THE SOVEREIGNTY OF THE SPIRIT

In preaching, Lloyd-Jones acknowledged the sovereign freedom of the Holy Spirit. The Spirit's divine path cannot be predicted nor controlled. "The power came, and the power was withdrawn. Such is the Lordship of the Spirit! You cannot command this blessing, you cannot order it; it is entirely the gift of God."[14] This uncontrollable activity of the Spirit adds to the inexplicable mystery of preaching.

For this reason, Lloyd-Jones said the pulpit is the most special place in which one can serve God. A preacher, he contended, never knows what to expect when he stands before the congregation to preach:

> The most romantic place on earth is the pulpit. I ascend the pulpit stairs Sunday after Sunday; I never know what is going to happen. I confess that I come expecting nothing; but suddenly the power is given. At other times I think I have a great deal because of my preparation; but, alas, I find there is no power in it. Thank God it is like that. I do my utmost, but he controls the supply and the power, he infuses it.[15]

When a Spirit-filled preacher is in the pulpit, Lloyd-Jones explained, he is spiritually elevated. He stated, "A preacher is taken up; he is in the realm of the Spirit and God is giving a message through this man to the people."[16] He asserted that the Spirit gives to the preacher unusual abilities that lie far beyond his natural talents. Lloyd-Jones puts it this way:

---

14. Ibid., 324.
15. D. Martyn Lloyd-Jones, *Spiritual Depression: Its Causes and Cures* (Grand Rapids, Mich.: Eerdmans, 1965), 299–300.
16. Lloyd-Jones, *Knowing the Times*, 276.

It gives clarity of thought, clarity of speech, ease of utterance, a great sense of authority and confidence as you are preaching, an awareness of power not your own thrilling through the whole of your being, and an indescribable sense of joy. You are a man "possessed," you are taken hold of and taken up. I like to put it like this—and I know of nothing on earth that is comparable to this feeling—that when this happens you have a feeling that you are not actually doing the preaching, you are looking on. You are looking on at yourself in amazement as this is happening. It is not your effort; you are just the instrument, the channel, the vehicle: and the Spirit is using you, and you are looking on in great enjoyment and astonishment.[17]

If this unction is the sovereign gift of the Spirit, Lloyd-Jones believed it is the preacher's responsibility to pray and ask for this divine power. God alone can give such might to His messengers. He urged all preachers:

Seek Him! . . . But go beyond seeking Him, expect Him. . . . Seek this power, expect this power, yearn for this power; and when the power comes yield to Him. . . . I am certain, as I have said several times before, that nothing but a return of this power of the Spirit

---

17. Lloyd-Jones, *Preaching and Preachers*, 324.

on our preaching is going to avail us anything. This makes true preaching, and it is the greatest need of all today—never more so.[18]

Lloyd-Jones was convinced that expository preaching should never be dry and lifeless. His burden was that those who preach the Word would know the power of the Spirit in their pulpit exposition. The people listening to a Spirit-filled preacher, he reasoned, will also sense the reality of what God is doing in the preacher. Lloyd-Jones explained:

> What about the people? They sense it at once; they can tell the difference immediately. They are gripped, they become serious, they are convicted, they are moved, they are humbled. Some are convicted of sin, others are lifted up to the heavens, anything may happen to any one of them. They know at once that something quite unusual and exceptional is happening. As a result they begin to delight in the things of God and they want more and more teaching.[19]

This is why numerous people made their way each Lord's Day to a church in the heart of London, where they listened to sermons lasting forty minutes to an hour. They knew God would be unusually present there. They discerned the power

---

18. Ibid., 325.
19. Ibid., 324–25.

of the Spirit upon the preaching of Lloyd-Jones. This antici-
pation created a deeper desire to know and live the truth.

THE EMPOWERMENT OF THE HOLY SPIRIT

Authoritative preaching, Lloyd-Jones claimed, "is God giving power, and enabling [him], through the Spirit . . . [to]
do this work in a manner that lifts it up beyond the efforts
and endeavors of man."[20] The power of God works within the
preacher in such preaching, energizing him to expound the
Scripture with an unusual ability beyond his own. He noted:

> True preaching, after all, is God acting. It is not just a
> man uttering words; it is God using him. He is being
> used of God. He is under the influence of the Holy
> Spirit; it is what Paul calls in 1 Corinthians 2 "preach-
> ing in demonstration of the Spirit of power." Or as he
> puts it in 1 Thessalonians 1:5: "Our gospel came not
> unto you in word only, but also in power, and in the
> Holy Ghost, and in much assurance. . . . " There it is
> and that is an essential element in true preaching.[21]

Lloyd-Jones acknowledged that the Spirit provides rapid
and expanded thought with deeper feelings and convictions
in the pulpit. He stated: "It is of the very essence of the act

---

20. Ibid., 305.
21. Ibid., 95.

of preaching—this freedom in your own mind and spirit, this being free to the influences of the Spirit upon you. If we believe in the Holy Spirit at all, we must believe that He is acting powerfully while we are engaged in this most serious and wonderful work."[22] He urged preachers to earnestly pray that God would "manifest His power in you and through you."[23] The Spirit must give both freedom and fervency in preaching so that the Word may run its course. Lloyd-Jones maintained: "Nothing but a return of this power of the Spirit on our preaching is going to avail us anything. This makes true preaching."[24] In short, Lloyd-Jones affirmed that if preaching is to know the blessing of God, it must have the power of God.

THE NECESSITY OF THE HOLY SPIRIT

Lloyd-Jones believed that without the Holy Spirit, there can be no real preaching. Preaching, to be sure, is a God-given ability. This is why no amount of natural ability will suffice for the lack of the Spirit's power. This is why Lloyd-Jones so emphasized the necessity of the Spirit in his ministry—and rightly so. He affirmed:

> Many terms can be used with respect to this God-given ability to preach. One quotation seems to me to sum it all up very well. Probably the first letter that

---

22. Ibid., 229.
23. Ibid., 325.
24. Ibid.

Paul ever wrote was to the church at Thessalonica, and in the first chapter of the first epistle, he reminds the believers of how the Gospel had come to them: "Our gospel came not unto you in word only, but also in power, and in the Holy Ghost, and in much assurance" (1 Thessalonians 1:5). Paul was saying: "I did the speaking, but it was not I. I was used." As he was speaking, he knew that he was merely the vehicle, the channel, the instrument that the Holy Spirit was using. He was taken up; he was out of himself; he was, as it were, possessed by the Spirit, and he knew that he was preaching with "much assurance."[25]

Even after the preparatory work has been completed and the sermon is being preached, the Spirit must still work in the preacher to deepen his insight into the text. He explained:

Preaching should be always under the Spirit—His power and control. . . . You will find that the Spirit Who has helped you in your preparation may now help you, while you are speaking, in an entirely new way, and open things out to you which you had not seen while you were preparing your sermon.[26]

Lloyd-Jones insisted that without the power of the Spirit,

---

25. Lloyd-Jones, *Courageous Christianity*, 191.
26. Lloyd-Jones, *Preaching and Preachers*, 85.

a man in the pulpit is merely reading his notes and repeating words. Quite simply, "If there is no power it is not preaching."[27] But where the Spirit is at work, God is present in power. Where the Spirit is at work, there is more than the mere speaking of words, but the influence of power upon both the preacher and his hearers. The inward ministry of the Holy Spirit, Lloyd-Jones believed, gives the preacher everything he needs to effectively proclaim the Word.

In his own preaching, Lloyd-Jones recognized a spontaneity of thought and clarity of expression as the Spirit worked in him. He stressed that it was often what he had not planned to say but declared in the pulpit that made the greatest impact upon his listeners. He noted: "One of the remarkable things about preaching is that often one finds that the best things one says are things that have not been premeditated, and were not even thought of in the preparation of the sermon, but are given while one is actually speaking and preaching."[28] As such, Lloyd-Jones believed that the preacher must never be restricted by his notes.

After having sufficiently prepared, the preacher is to exposit his biblical text in the power of the Spirit. God must grant the ability to speak clearly through His Word. This creates a great freedom in the preacher. Lloyd-Jones commented: "The great thing is freedom. I cannot over-emphasise this. It is of the very essence of the act of preaching—this freedom in

27. Ibid., 95.
28. Ibid., 84.

your own mind and spirit, this being free to the influences of the Spirit upon you."[29]

When the Spirit of God animates the preacher, he often adds to his notes. "If we believe in the Holy Spirit at all, we must believe that He is acting powerfully while we are engaged in this most serious and wonderful work. We must therefore be open to His influences."[30] In the Spirit's power, the preacher speaks what is fresh, applicable, and relevant to his hearers. This is why it is vitally important that the preacher understand the necessity of the Spirit in preaching.

THE 'DUAL ACTION' OF THE HOLY SPIRIT

With everything Lloyd-Jones believed regarding the unction of the Holy Spirit upon the preacher, he also believed such empowerment was not enough. The Spirit must also be doing something else within the hearers as they listen to the preaching of God's Word. He stated, "If the Holy Spirit only acted on the preacher, there would be no conversions."[31] In other words, merely being a Spirit-filled preacher is only the first step in producing soul-saving results. There must also be the convicting power of the Holy Spirit working within the hearts of the listeners.[32] Lloyd-Jones believed there to be, what he called, a "dual action," work of the Spirit. He said,

---

29. Ibid., 229.

30. Ibid.

31. Lloyd-Jones, *Courageous Christianity*, 192.

32. Ibid., 193.

This, then, is the dual action of the Spirit. He takes the preacher, the speaker, whether in a pulpit or in private, and gives this enabling. Then the Holy Spirit acts upon the ones who are listening and deals with their minds and hearts and wills. Both things happen at the same time.[33]

That the Holy Spirit is working within the hearts of the listeners should give the preacher that much more confidence that the results do not depend upon his abilities. As Lloyd-Jones stood to proclaim God's inerrant Word, he was aware of his need to be empowered by the Holy Spirit. He also was fully conscious that unless the Spirit took his words and drove them into the hearts of his congregation, like a nail into wood, there would be no salvation and no transformation.

Martyn Lloyd-Jones possessed many God-given gifts and abilities, yet he was fully aware that it wasn't those gifts that lay at the heart of his usefulness. He knew he had abilities, but he believed that it is only when God is pleased to work that eternal good is achieved. He was humbly aware that it was "not by might, nor by power, but by my Spirit, says the LORD of hosts" (Zech. 4:6 ESV).

Let us not be confident in our own natural abilities, oratorical talents, or skills of elocution, but let us depend fully upon the power of the Spirit to propel the Word of God as

---

33. Ibid.

it is preached into the hearts and minds of those listening. Therefore, being fully convinced that the Spirit "blows where he wishes" (John 3:8) will free us to proclaim the message of Scripture with boldness and clarity.

We Want Again
Lloyd-Joneses!

We do not stand that far removed from the time of Martyn Lloyd-Jones. In fact, there will be many who read these pages that were alive during the height of his ministry in London or who had the privilege of sitting under his preaching. To be sure, we stand in a period of history that is bereft of expository preaching, much as Lloyd-Jones did when he began his own preaching ministry. In many churches, entertainment has taken center stage, a message of prosperity has become dominant, and, sadly, clear biblical exposition is nearly extinct.

What are we to do? We must do as Lloyd-Jones did. We must capture the primacy and power of biblical preaching once again. There must be a decisive return to preaching that is Word-centered, God-exalting, Christ-centered, and Spirit-empowered. We need men who are committed to the difficult and laborious work of exposition. We need men who take apart Scripture, verse by verse, and preach it as a demonstration of the power of the Holy Spirit for the growth and holiness of God's people. In short, we need Lloyd-Joneses again to stand in pulpits across our land and unapologetically proclaim the Word of the living God.

Martyn Lloyd-Jones will have the final word here. What kind of preacher do we need today? This pulpiteer answers:

> The chief thing is the love of God, the love of souls, a knowledge of the Truth, and the Holy Spirit within you. These are the things that make the preacher. If he has the love of God in his heart, and if he has a love for God; if he has the love of the souls of men, and concern about them; if he knows the truth of the Scriptures; and has the Spirit of God within him, that man will preach.[1]

May Lloyd-Jones' description of the preacher be embodied in a new generation of gospel heralds in our day. We *do* want Lloyd-Joneses again. We *must* have Lloyd-Joneses again. And, by God's grace, we shall see them raised up again in this hour. May the Head of the church give us again an army of biblical expositors, men of God sold out for a new reformation.

Soli Deo gloria.

---

1. Lloyd-Jones, *Preaching and Preachers*, 120.

BIBLIOGRAPHY

Alexander, Eric J. Foreword to *The Cross: God's Way of Salvation*, by Martyn Lloyd-Jones. Edited by Christopher Catherwood. Wheaton, Ill.: Crossway, 1986.

Bailie, Ben. "Lloyd-Jones and the Demise of Preaching." In *Engaging with Martyn Lloyd-Jones,* edited by Andrew Atherstone and David Ceri Jones. Nottingham, England: InterVarsity, 2011.

Catherwood, Christopher. *Five Evangelical Leaders*. Wheaton, Ill.: Harold Shaw, 1985.

———, ed. *Martyn Lloyd-Jones: Chosen By God*. Westchester, Ill.: Crossway, 1986.

———. *Martyn Lloyd-Jones: A Family Portrait*. Grand Rapids, Mich.: Baker, 1994.

Daniel, Curt. *The History and Theology of Calvinism*. Springfield, Ill.: Reformed Bible Church, 2003.

Davies, Eryl. *Dr. D. Martyn Lloyd-Jones*. Darlington, England: Evangelical, 2011.

Duncan III, J. Ligon. "Some Things to Look For and Wrestle With." In *Preaching and Preachers: 40th Anniversary Edition,* by D. Martyn Lloyd-Jones. Grand Rapids, Mich.: Zondervan, 2009.

Haykin, Michael A.G. "From the Editor." *Eusebeia* 7 (Spring 2007): 3–4.

Hughes, Philip Edgcumbe. "The Theologian." In *Martyn Lloyd-Jones: Chosen By God*, edited by Christopher Catherwood. Westchester, Ill.: Crossway, 1986.

Lewis, Peter. "The Doctor as a Preacher." In *Martyn Lloyd-Jones: Chosen By God*, edited by Christopher Catherwood. Westchester, Ill.: Crossway, 1986.

Lloyd-Jones, D. Martyn. *The Assurance of Our Salvation: Exploring the Depth of Jesus' Prayer for His Own; Studies in John 17*. Wheaton, Ill.: Crossway, 2000.

———. *Authority.* 1958. Reprint, Edinburgh, Scotland: Banner of Truth, 1984.

———. *The Christ-Centered Preaching of Martyn Lloyd-Jones: Classic Sermons for the Church Today.* Edited by Elizabeth Catherwood and Christopher Catherwood. Wheaton, Ill.: Crossway, 2014.

———. *The Christian Soldier: An Exposition of Ephesians 6:10–20.* Grand Rapids, Mich.: Baker, 1977.

———. *Courageous Christianity.* Wheaton, Ill.: Crossway, 2001.

———. *Faith on Trial.* Clover, S.C.: Christian Heritage, 2008.

———. *God's Ultimate Purpose: An Exposition of Ephesians 1:1–23.* Grand Rapids, Mich.: Baker, 1978.

———. *God's Way of Reconciliation.* Grand Rapids, Mich.: Baker, 1972.

———. *God the Holy Spirit.* Wheaton, Ill.: Crossway, 1997.

———. *Great Doctrines of the Bible.* Wheaton, Ill.: Crossway, 2003.

———. *Knowing the Times.* Edinburgh, Scotland: Banner of Truth, 1989.

———. *Life in Christ: Studies in 1 John.* Wheaton, Ill.: Crossway, 2002.

———. *The Life of Peace.* Grand Rapids, Mich.: Baker, 1992.

———. *Old Testament Evangelistic Sermons.* Edinburgh, Scotland: Banner of Truth, 1995.

———. *The Plight of Man and the Power of God.* Grand Rapids, Mich.: Eerdmans, 1945.

———. *Preaching and Preachers.* Grand Rapids, Mich.: Zondervan, 1971.

———. "The Return to the Bible." *Eusebeia* 7 (Spring 2007): 7–14.

———. *Romans: Exposition of Chapter 3:20–4:25; Atonement and Justification.* Edinburgh, Scotland: Banner of Truth, 1970.

———. *Romans: Exposition of Chapter 9; God's Sovereign Purpose.* Edinburgh, Scotland: Banner of Truth, 1991.

———. *Romans: The Final Perseverance of the Saints; Exposition of Chapter 8:17–39.* Grand Rapids, Mich.: Zondervan, 1975.

———. *Spiritual Depression: Its Causes and Cures.* Grand Rapids, Mich.: Eerdmans, 1965.

———. *Studies in the Sermon on the Mount.* Grand Rapids, Mich.: Eerdmans, 1959.

Murray, Iain H. *D. Martyn Lloyd-Jones: The Fight of Faith, 1939–1981.* Edinburgh, Scotland: Banner of Truth, 1990.

———. *D. Martyn Lloyd-Jones: The First Forty Years, 1899–1939.* Edinburgh, Scotland: Banner of Truth, 1982.

———. *Evangelicalism Divided.* Edinburgh, Scotland: Banner of Truth, 2001.

———. *John MacArthur: Servant of the Word and Flock.* Edinburgh, Scotland: Banner of Truth, 2011.

———. *The Life of Martyn Lloyd-Jones, 1899–1981.* Edinburgh, Scotland: Banner of Truth, 2013.

———. *Lloyd-Jones: Messenger of Grace.* Edinburgh, Scotland: Banner of Truth, 2008.

Old, Hughes Oliphant. *The Reading and Preaching of the Scriptures in the Worship of the Christian Church, Vol. 6: The Modern Age.* Grand Rapids, Mich.: Eerdmans, 2007.

Piper, John, "Martyn Lloyd-Jones: The Preacher." In *Preaching and Preachers: 40th Anniversary Edition,* by D. Martyn Lloyd-Jones. Grand Rapids, Mich.: Zondervan, 2009.

Rusten, Michael, and Sharon O. Rusten. *The One Year Christian History.* Wheaton, Ill.: Tyndale House, 2003.

Turner, Charles, ed. *Chosen Vessels: Portraits of Ten Outstanding Christian Men.* Ann Arbor, Mich.: Vine, 1985.

INDEX

ABOUT THE AUTHOR

Dr. Steven J. Lawson is president of OnePassion Ministries, a ministry designed to bring about biblical reformation in the church today, and former senior pastor of Christ Fellowship Baptist Church in Mobile, Alabama. He served as a pastor for thirty-four years, having previously served in Arkansas and Alabama. He is a graduate of Texas Tech University (B.B.A.), Dallas Theological Seminary (Th.M.), and Reformed Theological Seminary (D.Min.).

Dr. Lawson is the author of nearly two dozen books, his most recent being *John Knox: Fearless Faith* and *In It to Win It: Pursuing Victory in the One Race That Really Counts*. His other books include *The Daring Mission of William Tyndale*; *Foundations of Grace* and *Pillars of Grace* from the Long Line of Godly Men series; *Famine in the Land: A Passionate Call to Expository Preaching*; *Psalms* volumes 1 and 2 and *Job* in the Holman Old Testament Commentary Series; *Made in Our Image*; and *Absolutely Sure*. His books have been translated into various languages, including Russian, Italian, Portuguese, Spanish, German, Albanian, and Indonesian. He has contributed articles to *Bibliotheca Sacra*, *The Southern Baptist Journal of Theology*, *Faith and Mission*, *Decision* magazine, *Discipleship Journal*, and *Tabletalk*, among other journals and magazines.

Dr. Lawson's pulpit ministry takes him around the world, including Russia, Ukraine, Wales, England, Germany, Italy, Switzerland, New Zealand, Japan, and to many conferences in the United States, including The Shepherd's Conference at Grace Community Church in Sun Valley, California.

He is a teaching fellow and board member for Ligonier Ministries and visiting professor for the Ligonier Academy of Biblical and Theological Studies. He also serves as professor of preaching and director of the doctor of ministry program at The Master's Seminary and as a member of the board of directors for The Master's College and Seminary. He hosts The Expositors' Conference at Christ Fellowship Baptist Church and has participated in the Distinguished Scholars Lecture Series at The Master's Seminary. He also serves on the advisory council for Samara Preachers' Institute and Theological Seminary in Samara, Russia.

Dr. Lawson and his wife, Anne, have three sons, Andrew, James, and John, and a daughter, Grace Anne.